How to Fix Meetings

How to Fix Meetings

Meet Less,
Focus on Outcomes
and Get Stuff Done

Graham Allcott
and Hayley Watts

ICON

Published in the UK and USA in 2021
by Icon Books Ltd, Omnibus Business Centre,
39–41 North Road, London N7 9DP
email: info@iconbooks.com
www.iconbooks.com

Sold in the UK, Europe and Asia
by Faber & Faber Ltd, Bloomsbury House,
74–77 Great Russell Street,
London WC1B 3DA or their agents

Distributed in the UK, Europe and Asia
by Grantham Book Services,
Trent Road, Grantham NG31 7XQ

Distributed in Australia and New Zealand
by Allen & Unwin Pty Ltd, PO Box 8500,
83 Alexander Street, Crows Nest, NSW 2065

Distributed in South Africa
by Jonathan Ball,
Office B4, The District,
41 Sir Lowry Road, Woodstock 7925

Distributed in India
by Penguin Books India,
7th Floor, Infinity Tower – C, DLF Cyber City,
Gurgaon 122002, Haryana

Distributed in the USA
by Publishers Group West,
1700 Fourth Street, Berkeley, CA 94710

Distributed in Canada
by Publishers Group Canada,
76 Stafford Street, Unit 300,
Toronto, Ontario M6J 2S1

ISBN: 978-178578-475-0

Typeset by Cecile Berbesi

Printed and bound in Great Britain
by Clays Ltd, Elcograf S.p.A.

ABOUT THE AUTHORS

GRAHAM ALLCOTT

Graham Allcott is a speaker, an entrepreneur and the founder of Think Productive, one of the world's leading providers of business productivity workshops and coaching. Think Productive's client list includes eBay, the Bill & Melinda Gates Foundation, Heineken and GlaxoSmithKline.

Think Productive workshops include:

How to be a Productivity Ninja
Getting Your Inbox to Zero
Email Etiquette
Fixing Meetings

Graham is the author of the international bestseller *How to be a Productivity Ninja*, as well as *A Practical Guide to Productivity* and *How to be a Study Ninja*. He is also host of the popular business podcast *Beyond Busy*.

Prior to founding Think Productive, Graham held various roles, including co-founder of Intervol, chief executive of Student Volunteering England and adviser to the UK government on youth and community issues.

Despite an intolerance of failure elsewhere in his life, he is an Aston Villa season ticket holder and an avid follower of the Toronto Blue Jays baseball team.

Graham lives in Brighton, UK.

HAYLEY WATTS

Hayley Watts has worked as a Productivity Ninja at Think Productive since 2014, where she is a coach and trainer. Prior to Think Productive, she spent years working with charities, businesses and statutory organisations, where she spent way too much time in ineffective meetings.

Hayley met Graham when they both worked in student unions after graduating, and when he founded Think Productive she asked him to run a training session for her staff. The Think Productive training changed Hayley's life, significantly reducing her stress levels. It wasn't long before she joined the team herself.

Outside of the working world, Hayley loves dancing of all kinds, a spot of yoga and walking her dog. She is a mum, a school governor and general organiser of stuff! Her favourite thing to do is get deeply engrossed in a good novel or go for long walks with her partner and friends.

CONTENTS

1.
WHY MEETINGS ARE BROKEN

THE PROBLEM WITH MEETINGS

'Let's have a meeting.' Four short words that conclude many a work conversation. What follows is often a sinking feeling. 'Ugh. Another meeting. There goes *another* hour of my life that I'll never get back, and *another* hour of my productivity down the drain.'

Well, the mission of this book is to spark change. Our goal is that the next time someone says: 'Let's have a meeting,' your immediate reaction is: 'Fantastic! What a brilliant opportunity to get things done!'

For the last decade or so, our company Think Productive has been working with some of the brightest and best organisations in the world, helping them to make space for what matters. That includes cutting down on unnecessary meetings and making sure that when a group of people *do* need to meet, it's as efficient, dynamic and productive as possible.

Our philosophy is pragmatic. We don't believe in four-hour work weeks or magic silver bullet solutions. We know that meetings can be important spaces to change the world, and that not every meeting is a waste of time. But we also know that every meeting has the *potential* to waste our precious time if it's not done right.

Productivity is about clearing the clutter to make space for the things that truly add value. So we start this book with two simple premises:

1. Meetings matter. Some of the most satisfying, company-changing, pace-setting or productivity-boosting moments we can remember in our working lives came in the middle of a well-executed meeting. You can probably think back to some of the defining 'moments of truth' in your own career and see the power that came from a group of people

together (physically or virtually) identifying a solution, or hitting on an idea, finally reaching consensus, or having that painful discussion so that you could all move on. Good meetings create a momentum that email and collaboration tools often cannot. And *great* meetings can even be powerful, life-affirming moments of human connection. If you can't think of a meeting you've experienced that fits that description, we know you'll start to see this in action by the time you've worked through the exercises in this book.

2. Lots of meetings don't matter at all. You can probably quite easily recall a great many moments spent in someone else's boring, frustrating and unproductive meeting. We know that most of the organisations we work with have too many meetings, and clients don't miss them when we help to cut a good chunk out of their schedule. Strangely, having fewer meetings also has a positive effect on the meetings that are left, giving everyone the time and headspace to make them more useful and fulfilling.

BAD MEETINGS WASTE OUR TIME

If you're tired of your diary being full of back-to-back, sub-optimal meetings, then you're not alone. A *Harvard Business Review* survey of senior managers in a range of industries found that 65% of people said meetings kept them from completing their own work, 71% said meetings were unproductive and inefficient, 64% said meetings came at the expense of deep thinking and 62% even said that meetings missed the opportunities to bring the team closer together (which is probably the number one argument you'll hear from back-to-back meeting apologists).[1] Reclaiming even just a small amount of those hours for you and your team members would be a huge productivity boost.

As so much time is wasted in meetings, it's no wonder that enthusiasm isn't at its highest when we get an email invitation for the next one – meeting fatigue is real. And it's a downwards spiral: the busier everyone becomes, the less time there is to make the next meeting any different, and the less effort you want to put in.

> **• REMEMBER •**
>
> Aim to do less meetings, but do them well. Done well, they can create real impact. Done badly, they are a drain on time and energy.

THE COST OF MEETINGS

Meetings are expensive. A study by the *Wall Street Journal* found that the average employee spends 31 hours a month in meetings, with more hours lost to meetings the more senior they are. CEOs typically spend 27 hours of their week in meetings (and their hours are expensive!).[2]

There are two costs to the company: the first is each person's salary as well as the costs of the space or online platform, the supporting infrastructure and so on; the second is the lost opportunities when more impactful work is neglected.

THE ATTENTION CRISIS

The challenge of productivity in the information age is how best to use our attention.

Do we have your complete attention right now? Take a moment to pause and contemplate that question. Be honest. We wouldn't be too surprised if the answer was 'no'. You have hundreds of things competing for your attention: from colleagues to phone notifications; from adverts to big ideas; from friends and family to your own inner monologue.

Attention – not time – is our most precious resource. It's the key to high performance and productivity in both work and life.

Organising and prioritising our thoughts brings the clarity needed for action, yet managers regularly tell us they view solo thinking-time as a luxury. But in a world where everyone's attention is so fragmented, we'd like to contend that it's an opportunity for competitive advantage. We overcome procrastination and come up with our best ideas when we make the space to think.

The same is true for great meetings. It's our ability to focus our attention – our hearts and minds, our problem-solving skills, our ideas – with other people that creates change, momentum and those 'moments of truth'.

Right now, we are living through an attention crisis. Technology and information overload play their part, training our attention to be more fragmented. You may think you have a fairly balanced relationship with your phone, but the science around what they do to our brains is pretty astounding. A recent study by the University of Texas at Austin found that a smartphone can sap attention even when it's not being used, even if it is on silent, and even when powered off and tucked away in a purse or briefcase.[3] And if you think you're good at ignoring your phone, you might be surprised to learn that even the notification noises, such as vibrations or alerts, are just as distracting for your brain as physically picking it up and using it.[4] This has dire consequences. One study found that the average British adult's attention span is now just five minutes and seven seconds, compared to twelve minutes a decade ago. It also found that younger people – traditionally thought of as having 'fresher' brain power – were outperformed by the over

50s, suggesting a link between lifestyle, phone usage, and wider attention span.[5]

What have you gained and lost over the last decade or so, as information overload has taken hold? You may love your phone and find the convenience far outweighs the negatives. You may find that you're regularly nagging yourself to make some changes and have a healthier relationship with technology or social media. What's clear is that the spaces in between activities are shrinking.

As a result, we have less time and space for thinking, reflection, noticing our own emotions, casual daydreaming and a myriad of other things. We're also more afraid of empty space. A joint study by Harvard and the University of Virginia found that one of the most terrifying things for people is being alone with their own thoughts, and that 67% of men would choose to self-administer electric shocks rather than be left alone in a room with nothing but their thoughts for fifteen minutes.[6]

Our need to be constantly connected to the outside world, checking our messages and notifications, can cause us to struggle to pay attention to our work, including the meetings we attend and the actions we should be completing. We need to make changes to improve both our productivity and our well-being.

THE MISSED OPPORTUNITY TO CREATE MAGIC

The frustrating thing is that in a world of fragmented attention, we need good meetings more than ever. Meetings should really be the force creating clarity, change, momentum, consensus and power in your team, your organisation, and indeed in the wider world too.

In our work, we have seen profound moments where previously conflicted teams have come together, and moments of inspiration that changed the direction of entire teams. We've also worked with leaders for whom good meeting practice was second nature, where even seemingly unmemorable meetings contributed to creating trust, accountability and respect within the team. These meetings often followed a particular structure to create a rhythm or ritual, and used techniques that we'll talk about throughout this book. But at their heart was something even more important: they were a place for truly listening to others.

Great leaders create a meeting environment where giving your fullest attention to your colleagues and to each tricky situation is a pre-requisite. It takes skill, practice and care, and it creates the kind of environment where standards are extremely high, where everyone is challenged to perform at their best and where ideas are scrutinised, disagreements are aired calmly and where empathy and understanding can easily flourish outside of the meeting space, seeping into the day-to-day culture of emails, Slack and rushed WhatsApp chats.

Humans – even the introverted ones – are tribal creatures. We feel good when we belong, when we are part of some bigger endeavour that we believe in, when we feel like our contribution is valued by others. This is why creating great meetings is as exciting as freeing our time from the terrible ones – because giving your fullest attention to someone is the most generous thing you can do in the world.

In fact, we believe that how humans 'do meetings' can also be part of a wider force for change. Learning to pay attention generously has obvious benefits to human interactions: it breeds the good forces that are lacking in our world, like empathy, vulnerability, kindness and connection. It lifts those around us, from co-workers to cashiers and cab drivers. Our invitation to you is that you don't just see this book and the principles within it as a way to make your 10am team meeting better. Focusing your attention can have profound effects on all areas of your – and others' – lives.

THE THINK PRODUCTIVE APPROACH

You may be wondering what experiences have led us, the authors, to a place where we're writing a book about meetings and attention. So just briefly, here's who we are and what we do.

THINK PRODUCTIVE: THE ATTENTION-MANAGEMENT COMPANY

Graham set up Think Productive in 2009, and since then has been working with some of the biggest, brightest and most interesting companies in the world. Before joining Think Productive, Hayley worked in a range of organisations, where she could see, from an outsider's perspective, the waste of time and energy that resulted from poor meeting practices. Hayley's particular interest within Think Productive is helping us to put that right for our clients. We've worked with teams at many of the biggest businesses on the planet: Amazon, Google, eBay, the Bill and Melinda Gates Foundation, Volkswagen, British Airways, PayPal and many more. We've also worked with smaller organisations, start-ups, charities and government departments. The point of this is not to brag about our CVs, but to say that we've seen a particularly wide range of working cultures: strict to supportive, controlling to loose, dictatorial to facilitative.

What unites all of the organisations we've worked with is that they've recognised, either through smart intuition, conversations with supervisors, or harsh employee engagement survey results, that their people are drowning – not just in information, but in tasks, many of which are complex and require decisions to be made around them. These tasks often compete with one another for time and attention, and for many people just deciding where to start and what to do next is a daunting decision. We've helped by running workshops showing employees how to get their email inboxes to zero, how to fix their meetings and of course how to get organised and ruthless like a Productivity Ninja.

Following the workshops, our clients often ensure that their employees maintain our key principles by sharing Graham's bestselling book, *How to be a Productivity Ninja*, among their teams. If you've not read it, we're going to quickly summarise the nine characteristics of the Productivity Ninja, which we will refer back to throughout the book. These characteristics form a toolbox of skills that you can use in different situations in your work (and life in general), providing a framework for efficient working habits and behaviours. It's likely there are some characteristics that you're already very good at, and others that it will be helpful to develop. If you're reading this because you're already a fan of *How to be a Productivity Ninja*, then you might want to skip the next couple of pages, but you might also like to use them as an opportunity for a quick reminder.

THE 9 CHARACTERISTICS OF THE PRODUCTIVITY NINJA

ZEN-LIKE CALM

As we've already alluded to here, our job is no longer about how we manage time, but how we manage our own attention. Zen-like calm is the mental state that produces focus and results. It's about being present, in-the-moment and doing one thing at a time. It's easier to do this when there's one big deadline looming (we can tell you this from experience as we write these words!) but much harder to do with 200 possibilities and competing priorities. The trick to this is getting all that stuff out of your head by using a 'second brain' which acts as your external memory (because our own brains are terrible for this!). This way, you can use your real brain for the stuff you are really good at: prioritisation, strategic thinking, decision-making and creativity. A second brain is like a more sophisticated to-do list. It could be written on paper or be an online tool. It brings different layers of thinking to your workload, enabling you to make better decisions about what to do next, and ensuring nothing is missed. More on this in Chapter 5.

RUTHLESSNESS

Having a ruthless mindset is vital for productivity and it's particularly pertinent to meetings, as you'll find out in the next chapter. Being ruthless with decision-making, saying 'no' to the stuff that gets in the way and recognising our own ability to procrastinate are all important components of ruthlessness. We will explain how to protect your attention by ruthlessly cutting yourself out of unnecessary and bad meetings, as this is vital to provide the space for the stuff that matters more.

WEAPON-SAVVY

Using tools in a savvy way, where you don't get distracted by shiny apps but use things that genuinely make your life easier, is of course a key aspect of productivity. The biggest opportunity for most people is to use an app as your 'second brain'. And when it comes to meetings, there are key tools like Doodle to help schedule them, or Meetings Timer to help keep track of the cost.

Since the Covid-19 crisis of 2020, meeting online has become the norm for many companies, with even the most face-to-face cultures embracing the technology. In this new era of online meetings, being weapon-savvy is as important as ever.

STEALTH & CAMOUFLAGE

Part of managing your attention is knowing when to be open and available versus when to be head-down and focused. One of the ideas we share a lot with our clients is 'tactical hiding': spending some time offline, making yourself deliberately less contactable, for the sole purpose of protecting the times in your day when you have what we call 'proactive attention' – your best energy and focus.

UNORTHODOXY

As you'll find out, we're also fans of doing things in unusual ways. Normal will get you average results. Normal is boring, too. Taking risks to try new things and mess with the status quo can help lead to more memorable meetings, spur the creativity for impactful solutions and keep work interesting.

AGILITY

In an age where shifting priorities can make work feel like it's in a constant state of flux, one of the most important skills, particularly for senior leaders, is the ability to be agile. We often need to drop everything to focus on some big catastrophe. If you're not in a state of emergency, one of the smartest things you can be doing is preparing for the next one – by keeping your 'second brain' and administrative systems lean and up to date, and by scanning the horizon with purpose, looking for where the next set of problems might come from. When you share your energy and attention with others in meetings, you will need agility to adapt to the different personalities and emotions of participants, and to help focus people's minds on the task at hand.

MINDFULNESS

Mindfulness meditation provides a route for us to experience what it's like to be truly in the moment. This is a vital skill for anyone looking to give their attention generously and to create meaningful conversations and interactions (as much in general life as in meetings!). Mindfulness is also very useful in helping us spot when our pesky 'lizard brain' – that irrational but highly tuned survivalist part of our brain – is freaking out or trying to encourage us to avoid the necessary conflict or discomfort in front of us. Being more mindful is often the best way to spot the more awkward, human elements that come into play when we're managing ourselves – those moments where we know exactly what we should be doing, but where procrastination and avoidance take hold and there's a gap between intention and action. (And don't try to convince us that you never procrastinate or avoid anything – it happens to us all, and it's nothing to be ashamed of, as long as we have the awareness to bring our minds back to focus when needed!)

PREPAREDNESS

As you're about to find out, great meetings – like all great work – rarely happen by accident. Planning ahead with care, being organised and getting the details right is all part of helping things go smoothly. Whether you love colour-coded folders or not, structure and order is what actually facilitates spontaneity and creativity. We like to see preparedness as giving your future self a gift: so when the pressure is on, you'll be really glad you already prepared the right documents and know where to find them now.

HUMAN, NOT SUPERHERO

With all the above characteristics under your belt, everyone else in the office will probably think you're some kind of superhero. But we know that high performers recognise they are human and embrace their fallibility. Not aiming to be perfect all the time makes our successes all the more remarkable and our failures all the more explainable. And when we recognise our weaknesses and accept imperfections, we pave the way for innovation and productivity to flourish.

HOW TO USE THIS BOOK

In this chapter, we've focused on why attention and mindset should be at the heart of fixing meetings. In the next chapter, we'll offer some solutions – both to help you cut down the time spent in bad meetings and to make the meetings you still need as productive as possible. Then in the following three chapters, we'll focus on all the practical stuff that you can do before, during and after meetings to promote the generosity of attention that can transform meetings, your team and even the world.

If your meetings don't change the world, or at the very least the world directly around you, something's not right. But you can make a difference.

Throughout the book there'll be practical exercises. We know lots of people skip the exercises, but please don't! We want to help you actually create change, rather than just read about the potential change. If you're pushed for time, focus on the exercises that either draw you in or repel you – we find that that's the best guide for where to put your attention.

> 'Never doubt that a small group of thoughtful, committed citizens can change the world; indeed, it's the only thing that ever has.' – Margaret Mead

And before we move on to the next chapter, it's over to you. Let's get thinking about your experiences of meetings so you can see what you're working with.

EXERCISE: HEAVEN AND HELL

One of the things we often ask clients in workshops is to think about their 'meeting heaven and meeting hell' – the best and worst meetings they've attended – and their general feelings about the role of meetings in the culture of their team or organisation. Spend a few minutes here considering your own answers to the following questions:

What you'll need:
Access to your calendar

How long it'll take:
About 15 minutes

Mindset:
Reflective

Meeting heaven:

▶ What was the last truly great meeting you went to? What made it great?

▶ When you think of someone who holds great meetings, who do you think of? What exactly do they do to make them great?

▶ Can you think of a time your own workload became clearer or easier as a result of a meeting? Why did that happen?

Meeting hell:

▶ What was the ratio of useful to less-than-useful meetings you went to in the last week?

▶ What are the hallmarks of a terrible meeting for you?

▶ What would you be doing instead if no meetings were allowed on Mondays, Tuesdays and Thursdays, and you suddenly had the whole of those days free in your calendar?

YOU WILL KNOW THAT YOU ARE FIXING MEETINGS WHEN:

▶ You aren't spending all of your days in back-to-back meetings.

▶ Meetings aren't always scheduled for an hour; in fact, they are as short as can be.

▶ The meetings you attended last week were a priority over the work you didn't get finished.

2.
THE SOLUTION

It would have been easier for us to write a book that claimed that every single meeting was equally worthwhile and simply focus on 'how to make them all brilliant'. It's also pretty easy to call a 'meetings amnesty' and declare no one should ever spend time in a meeting again. If only life and work were as simple as they seem in most management and self-help books!

The truth, of course, lies in the messy middle. Our approach is about finding the balance between the magic of frenetic collaboration and the magic of quiet and determined focus. Why? Because sometimes productivity is the result of the brilliant hive mind of a meeting, and sometimes it is the result of ignoring the rest of the world and getting stuff done. The sweet spot is between these two forces – and managing our attention in such a way that serves the wider goal we're trying to accomplish, rather than getting bogged down in the process of how to do it.

In this chapter, we're taking inspiration from the ancient Chinese dualist philosophy of yin and yang and will show you how to adopt this approach to your meetings. We'll cover the mindset and behaviours that we've found to be most effective, so that you can see how these principles inform the rest of the more practical chapters that follow. You can think of this chapter as a general outline before we get into the nitty-gritty details.

ATTENTION MANAGEMENT

It's often said that time is our most precious resource, but that's not true: attention is a more precious resource than time. We all have the same number of hours in a day, but not all of those hours give us the fullest energy and highest ability to focus on difficult or challenging tasks. Most people have two or three hours a day where their attention is at its peak. We call this proactive attention.

Step one in great attention management is developing the self-awareness to know which parts of the day are giving us that proactive attention and which hours of the day give us the opposite – sluggish and sub-optimal 'inactive attention'. (We've all been there. The slump hours where it feels like all you're doing is staring blankly at a screen.) Step two, of course, is to allocate the right kinds of work based on these differing levels of attention.

There will of course be hours of your best attention that feel like they're held hostage – lost to someone else's extremely unproductive meeting. Ninja-level productivity for you, and better still, ensuring a high-performing team of people around you, is about questioning the status quo, being a positive disruptor and not settling for inefficient ways of working. It's about asking good questions in an effort to reclaim this attention for great work. And sometimes it's about 'going dark', staying out of the way, or blocking out bits of our calendar so that these kinds of derailments are kept to a minimum (it's usually not the most politically-savvy move to try and eliminate them completely – it's about choosing your battles).

DEEP WORK

Cal Newport coined the term 'Deep Work' to describe this battle to reclaim our attention and stay productive. He shuns meetings, social media, email and other distractions – shallow activities that often skirt around an issue or talk about quality work, rather than actually *being* quality work – to spend as much time putting his mind and his attention to complex problems or deep creativity. He spends time in what he calls 'monk mode', with no connectivity to the outside world. We've noticed over the years that this is one of the practices that our clients find the most difficult to emulate, but when they do, the result is off-the-scale productivity. Newport also argues that as the robots take over, the biggest competitive advantage in the future of work will be our ability to hold our attention on things and think clearly. Given what we do at Think Productive, we clearly agree with his assessment.

DEEP LISTENING

There are also, of course, times when we need to 'go deep' in a different way. Paying deep attention to the needs of our colleagues, focusing on problems or issues and listening actively; these are all things that promote the harmony, trust and co-operation that every team needs to succeed. In fact, in a world that seems to move too fast to care about us, showing compassion for those around us is not just an essential part of teamwork, it's one of the most underrated business strategies there is. Think about it. It's often the evil mavericks who get the headlines, but the real heroes of companies and our economy are all those managers that you've loved working with in your career – the good men and women who had your back, acted as a sounding board and helped you grow. One of the most important aspects of leadership and management is listening to your people. And in our experience, what most of the great leaders have in common is that they create an environment that encourages everyone to stop and listen, no matter how frantic things seem.

Deep listening is often the best problem-solving tool there is, and in fast-paced, seemingly uncaring organisational cultures, kindness is also a radical act. By managing our attention, by listening to people, by focusing on one thing at a time, we can begin to change our behaviour both in and out of meetings. It's what high performers do when they are working at their very best.

BALANCING ACT

This brings us back to the balance. With only deep work, we'd end up with a team of mavericks who hated each other whenever they needed to work together. With only deep listening, we'd end up with a group therapy session. Treading the fine line down the middle, keeping both in balance, is the source of great productivity.

On understanding this, the next step as leaders and colleagues is to be sensitive to the fact that people need the autonomy to make their own decisions about where their attention goes, as well as sometimes needing to compromise their best attention for the good of the collective. Leaders or high performers need to generate more conversations about how each member of the team can best manage their attention. This includes talking about how and when you schedule meetings, the best times in the day for interruptions and discussion versus the time to be 'heads down' in the deep work, the agility to change the schedules regularly to suit the need, and so on. So allow us to introduce the yin and yang of meetings, which we hope will be a useful concept to help you navigate your own attention, as well as lead others to do the same.

THE YIN AND YANG OF MEETINGS

The ancient Chinese dualist philosophy symbol of yin and yang holds some profound truths. It tells us that there are different, opposing energies in the universe. Light and dark, fire and water, birth and death and so on. In the symbol, these two opposing forces – the yin and the yang – are represented as the opposite of each other, but they also both contain the seed of the other. Think of *Star Wars*: Luke Skywalker has at the back of his mind that he could be drawn to the dark side because of his father, whereas Darth Vader, as we all know, started out life as a Jedi. Both characters contain the seed of the other, opposite force, and depend on each other. This is what makes us interested in the story. Yin and yang aren't about stark opposites, they're about how opposing forces are interdependent, complementary and connected. (We can hazard a guess that a film that just said 'Here's Luke Skywalker. He was a good guy. There was nothing to fight against' wouldn't be one of the most successful movie franchises of all time.)

Yin is the more passive, receptive, softer energy. It's what happens in the shadows as opposed to the bright light. In business, yin energy brings us new ideas, intuition and discovery as well as important qualities for the harmony of team dynamics. Yin energy helps us to listen and makes sure that we get the best contributions from everybody.

Yang is the more active, aggressive energy. When we foster the yang energy we create targets, focus on growth, get stuff done and pursue our goals with ambition and vigour. Yang can be fiery and verges on destructive at times, but it can also be important to make sure we drive things forward.

It's the balance of these things that matters, in all working environments: if all we have is yin, the office would be a nice place to hang out, but we probably wouldn't get much done. If all we have is yang, then all that thoughtless aggressive growth would either tear everything apart or pull us in a million chaotic directions. We've all experienced leaders who are too 'wishy-washy' and overly facilitative, or too direct and task-driven but lacking in people skills. To succeed, each needs a seed of the other.

When we first started working with clients, running workshops on the topic of How to Fix Meetings, two seemingly contradictory statements kept coming up, again and again, and these are the two truths that we are trying to hold in balance:

1. Meetings matter because they are precious spaces to share our attention to make change.

2. Most meetings don't matter at all and they are a waste of the precious time that could be used for action.

YIN BEHAVIOURS FOR MEETINGS

ZEN-LIKE CALM

Being zen-like is all about separating the thinking from the doing: the art of thinking clearly (which in turn breeds the momentum for action and productivity) requires us to mentally 'clear the decks' and keep focused. Keeping a whole bunch of information in your head, or succumbing to digital distractions, is the quickest way to start feeling overwhelmed. We're the most productive when we're the most present and focused (think of what happens when you're on a deadline – it forces you to abandon a lot of the other things you might think about or distract yourself with, because the deadline gives you clarity that you're doing the right thing in that moment). In meetings, the same focus and zen-like calm will help you to fully participate and honour the contributions of others.

Being fully present in a meeting means:

▶ Putting all of your attention and focus in the room, whether that's physical or online.

▶ Not checking messages, or being distracted by concerns unrelated to the current meeting.

▶ Ensuring the meeting stays true to its core purpose (we'll come to the idea of purpose statements later).

▶ Recognising the subtexts, emotions and 'under the table' or off-screen battles that might be going on in the discussion – and doing as much as possible to either acknowledge these, or bring them above the table so that everyone can discuss them properly.

▶ Communicating on an emotional, values-level as much as on a productive or process-level.

▶ Respecting the contributions of everyone within the meeting.

MINDFULNESS

Mindfulness is also about being in the moment, and practices like meditation or yoga can be extremely valuable in helping us be more aware of what's going on in our own heads. All those nagging doubts, anxieties and self-talk nightmares get exposed, and scary as they are to confront, we usually find that when we can understand what is happening in our brains, we can learn how to stop derailing ourselves through procrastination and fear.

Often, when we feel emotionally vulnerable in meetings – threatened, isolated, challenged or aggrieved – it's tempting to lash out, to say things with a hotter head than is necessary and ultimately cause ill-feeling or disharmony (for no productive reason). Recognising our own emotions by being mindful and present helps us to regulate them and reduce the likelihood of our otherwise fantastic contributions being derailed. It's important to cultivate the humility to own up when things get out of hand, and to call out our own bad attitudes or reckless reactions.

If you're having an emotional response to a certain topic or challenge, the chances are you're not alone and it might be helpful to raise it. Likewise, it's helpful sometimes to just tune into whatever those specific thoughts are, acknowledge them in that moment with yourself, and move beyond them.

VALUING PEOPLE

At their best, meetings should be about human connections, recognising the emotional aspects of work and working together. It's easier to focus on the form of a meeting – the agenda, the timings, the shape of the answers – than it is to focus on the spirit. A lot of people are uncomfortable with 'spirit', values, emotions and stuff that feels too 'touchy-feely'. But if you want to create harmony and consensus, or create a culture of leadership where people take initiative not just direction, then being in touch with the team as people and knowing their values really matters.

Kindness and generosity can be intensely productive. They are brilliant ways to create empathy and connection. Generosity of attention and praise in meetings, for example, takes a little care and thought but can make all the difference.

One of the kindest things you can do for someone is listen to them. Really listen to them. We are now so used to the idea that everyone's attention is fragmented and distracted that it can be a deep and powerful experience to give and receive full attention. When you're in a conversation, try to be deeply *in* the conversation. Go all in. This requires space: space in your own head because you've organised your own thoughts, space in the conversation because you don't have a hundred competing voices, and space in the meeting because you don't have someone doing the yang thing of rushing the discussion forward before important things have been said.

Going deep also means acknowledging that sometimes conflict and disagreement is an important part of the process. As a meeting chair or facilitator, you may need to recognise that people have different thresholds of comfort with conflict. Phrases like 'OK, we need to have the awkward conversation' or 'it would be great to understand everyone's views and feelings on this' can help everyone to relax and creates a safe environment for the healthy discussion of conflict.

If this all sounds a bit inaccessible – a bit hippy-ish, even – then don't worry. There are loads of practical things you can do at every stage of the process that will invite the yin energy into your meetings. Whatever your role in a meeting, there are a few questions that might initially be helpful to guide your approach.

As a chair, facilitator or meeting organiser:

▶ What can I do to help the most fully present version of each participant show up to the meeting? How can I promote and foster honest appraisal of the issues rather than group-think or bravado?

▶ How can I ensure people feel relaxed, happy and playful (these are the opposites of feeling stressed and stuck in negative or unconstructive states)?

▶ What can I do, practically, to remind others of the bigger picture?

▶ Who might be really annoyed, hurt or threatened by the potential outcome of this meeting? What can I do before the meeting starts to help them anticipate and react?

As a meeting participant[1]:

▶ What is being said between the words of this meeting?

▶ How can I acknowledge and 'bring to the table' the stuff that currently feels like it's being said under the table?

▶ What's the courageous thing that needs to be said but no one is prepared to say? Why not me?

PUTTING IT INTO PRACTICE

Meetings start and end with people. The 'people stuff' can be tricky or awkward (especially to us Brits!) but a little investment in this can bring huge results.

All's well that starts well

Beginning your meetings with yin energy sets the tone and creates the space. It puts everyone at ease and allows them to participate fully. Here are some simple ways to start a meeting with the right tone:

▶ Welcome all participants. Not just saying the words and going through the motions, but being truly grateful to have all these specific people in the room with you.

▶ Start with an 'opening round', so that everyone gets a first chance to speak, on a topic that feels familiar to them (a quick sharing of good news, names and roles etc.).

▶ Start with a recap. Many avoid this as a way to start a meeting, and no doubt part of your brain will be screaming 'but everyone knows this already!' Do it anyway. Recap the purpose of the meeting, the progress so far, the problem you're trying to solve, and why you've asked these particular people here (name-checking them individually to ensure everyone feels valued).

All's well that ends well

Starting your meeting well sets the tone for the meeting. Ending the meeting well sets the tone for action. Like good speeches, the bits we tend to remember are the first few words and the last few words. What do you want these people to be carrying in their minds as they leave your meeting? What are the key things they need to feel, think about or do *as a result* of the meeting? Again, there are some simple things you can do here (and there're loads more practical ideas like this coming up in the next chapters):

▶ End with a thank you and a call to action. Value the time and input. Value the honesty and ideas.

▶ End with a 'closing round'. If you're the chair or facilitator, you might want to have the last word, but immediately before this, give everyone else their own last word too. A simple one-word summary can be a quick and easy way to do this. Or ask people to say in a few words what they're looking forward to or what they've enjoyed.

▶ End with a recap. Paint the positive picture of what the resulting actions will achieve.

THE SEED OF YANG IN YIN

Of course, meetings can't just be full of the 'touchy-feely stuff'. Meetings should also get results. There needs to be a focus on outcomes and a driving of the conversation towards those. As with yin and yang philosophy, there needs to be a seed of the opposite force in each side.

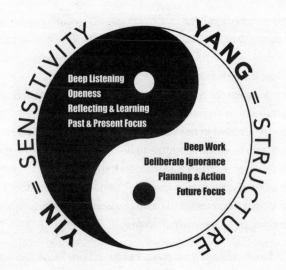

In the middle of a period of deep listening, we need an eye on the time. We need a structure: an agenda, perhaps timed items, space for comfort breaks and other practicalities, and so on. And the end of every meeting should be a crescendo of yang: the writing down of actions, a focus on the future and what things will actually get *done* as a result of all this talking.

YANG BEHAVIOURS FOR MEETINGS

RUTHLESSNESS: THE ART OF DELIBERATE IGNORANCE

Ruthlessness isn't about being a candidate on *The Apprentice* or a mean business-person stereotype, it's about starting at the desired result and working backwards from there. Ruthlessness means deliberate ignorance in order to protect our attention. This isn't a selfish act: it is necessary in an age of information overload in order to be creative and make things happen. It also means saying 'No' to many of the demands on our time, energy and attention. Saying no can be difficult, so here are some pointers to help.

Saying no to ourselves

It can be tricky to be ruthless with ourselves – we want to do a good job, work well with others and excel. But there are occasions where these desires get in the way of focusing our energy and attention in the places where we can make the most difference. We need to be able to say no to ourselves. It's human nature to feel a sense of duty or get excited in conversation with someone, and before you know it, you're committed to things that you really should have said no to. Practice the slow yes and the quick no. Ask, with every single thing, 'Is this really worth doing? Does it add enough value to the things that matter the most? Will it make a positive impact on what I want to achieve (whether that be financial or otherwise)?' If the answer isn't a clear 'hell yeah' then you should probably think again before committing. Sometimes an exciting idea is brought up, but on consideration, it isn't a priority, or it won't make an improvement for a significant number of people. There is nothing wrong with noting this idea down and coming back to it at a later date, but we want to encourage you to get ruthless and do the stuff that will create the most positive change rather than committing to every opportunity.

Of course, some meetings feel like they're huge opportunities even if they don't necessarily pertain to our biggest priorities. It can be tempting to fill up our diaries with meetings that we've accepted because we felt flattered

'The difference between successful people and really successful people is that really successful people say no to almost everything.'
– Warren Buffett

to be invited, or events we've said yes to because of a vague fear of missing out. Neither of these things alone are good reasons to say yes.

Don't go to most meetings

We of course know that it is not always possible to avoid meetings. There may be good political reasons why you need to show your face at a meeting: you may feel under obligation and certain meetings are simply unavoidable. But think about it this way: if your life depended on you having two hours free that are currently booked in for a meeting, you'd find a way to avoid it. Here are a few ways to start attending less:

▶ The one in three strategy. For regular meetings, such as team meetings, 'all hands' and so on, you won't fall massively behind by missing one every now and again. Let's face it, can you remember who was missing last time? Be strategic and choose the times to sneak off. We've both at different times in our careers adopted versions of the 'miss one in every three' strategy. Simple, but effective.

▶ Sending a colleague. Again, politically, there can be problems with sending a junior colleague to certain meetings on your behalf. But, there can also be benefits – it can allow your colleagues a chance to see the organisation through your eyes and to get to know some different people. Like the one in three strategy, this is something to be used sparingly, but it's a good way to reclaim some time.

▶ Sneaky Work Travelling is generally a great excuse to be out of the office and away from the perils of attention-sapping meetings. Strategically scheduling travel so that you have one appointment placed in the middle of a day can buy you a couple of hours of work-from-home time before you head out, or you can finish the appointment and then sit in a coffee shop to catch your breath, follow up or get some work done rather than risk heading straight back to the office. It's much easier to schedule a little bit of extra 'sneaky work time' around travelling to an appointment than it is to reclaim an hour's peace and quiet to concentrate in the middle of the average office day.

'Meetings are a symptom of bad organisation,
the fewer the better.' – Peter Drucker

Magic words

In psychological experiments, it's been found that using the word 'because' following your point is more likely to make people agree with you. Adding a plausible reason for why you can't say yes to something is obviously useful, but the science reveals that you don't even need to be that convincing – people often feel nervous to question the reasoning of others, and it's simply the word 'because' that makes all the difference.[2] Likewise, the word 'unfortunately' can add an air of inevitability to an answer, ending the conversation.

Personal policies

Saying no to a meeting or potential commitment because of a generic 'personal policy' rather than specifically to that request, is also a useful tool. For example, we both live about an hour from London, where we're often invited to meet people for coffee or attend events. We've found that saying 'I've used up my London days this month' is better than simply turning down a meeting request. Your personal policies could be anything from the time you allocate each year to pro bono work, the amount of money you give to charity, the type of work you've decided to focus on, the amount of travel you do and so on. The point is to be clear on what's appropriate and balanced for you, and set some boundaries – then let those boundaries make your decisions for you.

Here are some examples of personal policies that can help you to make space for the deep work, as well as making space for the right meetings. (Note: not all of these will apply to you, and you definitely don't need to try them all!):

▶ Open-door hours or 'manager-surgery hours' (this is a smart plan for a lot of managers, because open-door hours also allows for the possibility of *closed*-door hours).

▶ A set number of travel days or office days per week or month.

▶ No meetings in the morning/afternoon (e.g. Graham's meeting/collaboration windows are 2–5pm, Monday to Thursday).

▶ A set number of meeting hours per week. Imagine if everyone did this, and you could, in effect, trade hours of your time for hours of other peoples' – the scarcity of the commodity would make everyone think more carefully about meetings.

▶ A set amount of pro bono time, or time spent on non-core projects to help others in the organisation.

▶ Specific family/social time (set as a minimum, not a maximum!).

▶ Rules around particular projects (particularly good for freelancers) – for example, 'I don't do any work for free, for the exposure', or 'I only work with organisations or on projects that fit these criteria, which I've written up on my website as a handy guide'.

Project Magenta

The first rule of 'Project Magenta' is you must not talk about Project Magenta. Just calmly add it to your calendar. The idea here is that if your time is constantly getting booked up by colleagues sending you meeting requests, and those colleagues don't respect things like 'personal planning time' or 'catch-up time' or 'email processing', then you use this as your code name to signify a block of time where you will not be disrupted. Since your colleagues won't know what it is, they're unlikely to question its importance.

Guest appearances

With long meetings, it can often feel like your presence or input is only really needed for one or two of the agenda items and the rest feel less relevant. For these kinds of meetings, try having a conversation with the organiser beforehand, suggesting, 'I don't think I can make it to the whole thing, but how about I come just for the morning/come just for my item' or 'What time will that agenda point be covered, so I can log in then?'.

The small but helpful no

If you can't take on the whole assignment that you've been presented with, perhaps you can suggest someone else who might be better placed. (Obviously this one isn't always possible, especially if it really should be you!). Or rather than spend a day on the task, you can offer to spend half an hour over coffee giving the person who is asking for your help the benefit of your previous experience, in a bid to make their job easier?

If the person asking for input is someone you directly manage, it's worth asking yourself if you have become a bottleneck. If this is the case, look for ways to reduce the expectations so that the task is smaller and easier (bearing in mind they might be feeling more pressure or have a higher definition of success than is actually needed). You might want to direct them to someone else who can provide training or coaching in this area rather than getting involved in the detail yourself.

Interruptions

Finally, we need to say no to so many of the things that will impede our attention and focus. Turning off notifications on phones, email and messaging software is a good example. Making one big, positive decision to turn these things off is in effect saying no to hundreds of small daily interruptions that can make a big dent on our productivity.

It's also worth talking about open plan offices here. One of the regular complaints we get from people during workshops is that office interruptions are wasting their time. We get it. Open plan offices are, in our view, great for collaboration and socialising (and of course for saving money on office space), but they are not so good for productivity. Thankfully, there is a way out. It's usually got a big green sign above it that says 'exit'! So take charge of the situation. Spend a regular day each week or month working from home, so that you get a chance to get your head down and really focus. If that doesn't work for you, you can spend an hour each day working from the coffee shop or canteen. Being ruthless means making tough decisions, including making yourself deliberately a little less available, with the confidence that this is what's best for greater productivity.

> **• REMEMBER •**
>
> It's OK not to go to every meeting that you are invited to. Saying yes is saying no to other ways of using your attention.

EXERCISE: THE 'DELETE A DAY' CHALLENGE

Want to be a ruthlessness hero? How about we delete some meetings from your schedule? Yes, right now. Let's do this. We're going to reclaim seven hours of time – equivalent to a full day of back-to-back meetings – from your calendar.

What you'll need:
Your calendar/email

How long it'll take:
20 minutes

Mindset:
Ruthlessness

The aim is to save seven hours of meetings for you and your colleagues. So, for example, if you have a one-hour meeting with two colleagues, that's a total of three hours of time. If you have an hours' meeting with several colleagues and you're just going to send apologies but the meeting still goes ahead, well you've still saved an hour. If you have seven people sitting down for an hour and you can turn that into just a decisive email instead, then you've achieved the seven hours in one hit.

Step one: look at your calendar. Look first for the meetings where you're the organiser, or where you have some influence over who is attending. Can you cancel? Can you reduce the number of people you've invited (sent with a nice email explaining why – they'll usually be delighted to get the time back and will probably buy you cookies).

Step two: look next at the meetings where you're simply an attendee. Can you find a way to get out of attending? If it's a regular meeting and you need to be there this week, can you slip out of next week's? (Use the one in three rule here.)

Step three: if you can't outright cancel a particular meeting, can you make it shorter? If you change a meeting for eight people from two hours to 90 minutes, you've just saved four hours.

Step four: bask in the glory of reclaiming a day of time for you and your team.

Step five: if you're feeling brave, share the good news with colleagues that you've just completed the challenge. You might find that others take up the mantle, and some of the other meetings in your calendar may start mysteriously shrinking.

How did that feel? If you have a lot of autonomy over your own diary and send a lot of meeting invites, you might feel like deleting a day's worth of meetings was an easy thing to achieve. If you're someone who doesn't have so much control, perhaps it was a little harder. We'd suggest this is a good ruthless discipline to get into on a regular basis – and the easier you found it, the more often we'd suggest running through your calendar and clearing time for the yang energy and the deep work that will follow.

Preparedness

It's much easier to say no to things when you're clear on what you've already said yes to. In fact, having an up-to-date list of all your projects and actions is really empowering when it comes to channelling yang energy and being decisive. It means you and your boss can have an objective conversation about renegotiating your workload to fit in a new commitment, rather than a subjective one where it feels like they're judging whether you're a hard enough worker, with you responding by adding to your to-do list.

Preparedness is also a key part of the Productivity Ninja philosophy. It's amazing just how few of the people that we meet in our workshops can actually say they have a fully up-to-date to-do list. Even rarer is the idea of the Projects List, where you can see the bigger picture. Best practice would say you should also keep a Waiting List to keep track of the things you've delegated to others. These simple structures help us to feel in control and generate momentum – because if you've got a good list of all of your actions, there's always something you can get on with, even in the worst hours of lowly 'inactive attention'. Preparedness is clarity; clarity is halfway to done.

No agenda, no meeting

So many meetings are a waste of time because they're badly thought-out, or just not thought-out at all. It should be your personal mission to say no to any meeting that's not been properly prepared for, or that doesn't have an agenda. If you're invited to a meeting, ask to see the agenda before you can confirm attendance. If you've not seen an agenda, how can you possibly know if it's worthy of your time and attention? While this philosophy can seem a little aggressive at first, it can quickly spread to those around you – which of course means that someone will inevitably challenge *you* if you've organised a meeting without an agenda. The next level up on the same rule is that you only attend a meeting if it has both an agenda *and* a purpose statement, but more about those later!

NEXT PHYSICAL ACTION

The idea of the 'next physical action' is a key part of what we teach. Whenever you've got a task that needs to be done, try to picture yourself making a start. Often (and especially with new activities) we get stuck because we don't know what that first action looks like. Imagining yourself emailing or talking to someone or mind-mapping is much more useful than writing down 'get started with XYZ project' and expecting your brain to miraculously pick that off the to-do list and work magic with it. Getting into the habit of being detailed in the language you use with yourself is also a great practice for meetings. End every meeting with questions, focusing on actions with yang energy:

▶ OK, what's the next physical action here?

▶ Who's going to own this and be accountable?

▶ What will we be able to measure as progress, and by when?

It's amazing how we can all leave the same meeting feeling like there was a total consensus, only to discover that there was a huge gulf in expectations because specific actions weren't discussed, leading to problems further down the line.

Getting into this mindset takes a while. It requires being annoyingly specific and detailed in the language that we use with ourselves. It can seem like pedantry to colleagues sometimes. But once you see the benefits of clarity, it's difficult to imagine working in any other way again. The more you think about your work – and capture the specificity of what's ahead – the easier the work itself becomes.

CHANGING CULTURE

Being ruthless is a great personal survival tool. It allows you to rail against unproductive cultures that prevent rather than promote productivity. But what if you could also start to change the culture within your company, so that things weren't always so difficult in the first place? How about turning the odds in your favour, rather than feeling like you're constantly fighting a losing battle? The following ideas are all about changing culture, messing with what's accepted and above all bringing the focus back to the productivity of meetings, not the standard of the biscuits.

SET A TIME CHALLENGE

Parkinson's law is one of the most famous productivity rules. It says 'work expands so as to fill the time available'. We believe this is particularly true when you put a group of people together, with the purpose of discussing or agreeing on a certain topic. Most meetings are arranged for one hour or half an hour purely because they've been set up using a shared calendar on Microsoft Outlook with these timings as the default settings. You can, of course, have a 42-minute meeting, but you'd have to type in the timings of that, which would take all of eight seconds. So, twenty minutes of everyone's time is wasted because no one thought to break with the convention. If you're the organiser of a meeting, use a bit of unorthodoxy. Set it to last for 42 minutes instead of an hour. Or one hour and eighteen minutes instead of one hour and 30 minutes. These tiny changes will stand out. Not only will your meetings be shorter, allowing you to reclaim time in your day, but they will appear different and hence purposeful.

Alternatively, set a meeting for a conventional time, such as one hour and 30 minutes, but then start it off with a difference, saying 'OK, I know we're all busy. I'm setting you all a challenge. Let's get this done in an hour or less, rather than taking the full 90 minutes.' Everyone will love getting that time back.

POSITIVE DISRUPTION

As a general rule, the larger an organisation becomes, the slower it is to change. Organisations are an exaggerated version of people – they become stuck in their ways. Even tiny organisations with just a handful of people can get into a mode of comfort that doesn't promote continuous improvement. With this in mind, it's important to take it upon ourselves to mess things up a bit. Positive disruption is about asking the tough, challenging questions. It's about never settling for 'this is the way we do things around here', because there is always more to gain, always things that can be improved and new things that can be learned. Being the annoying person who's challenging the status quo can be a tough place to be, but remember that you are doing it with the purpose of improving productivity for all.

When it comes to disrupting meetings, why not instigate a new format, such as a huddle or a silent meeting (more on those later). You could arrange a walking meeting or an outdoor meeting, or even one in the pub, rather than one in the same stuffy meeting room you use over and over again. Or you could try committing you and your team to a week of being meeting-free.

Sometimes you won't know what works best until you try a few things out. The point is getting comfortable with the idea of experimenting – allowing room for failure and learning, which are key ingredients for success.

BLOW SH*T UP

'Blow sh*t up' is one of the corporate values of the craft beer company, BrewDog. Love them or hate them (or both) they're one of the fastest-growing companies in their market. As well as occasionally taking their whole team outside to literally blow stuff up, the mentality is one that they use to encourage everyone to stay curious and ensure nothing gets too comfortable.

At Think Productive, we often have an agenda item on our away days called 'Blow sh*t up, kill the sacred cows and truth amnesties'. Everyone is allowed to write down anything they think is unproductive or a waste of time in the way we operate as a company. Even if your team can't think of anything (and in our experience that's rare!), doing this exercise is really helpful to focus everyone's minds on what's effective and a good use of time and energy. We facilitate this with Post-it Notes so that everyone can submit their ideas anonymously. It encourages our team to speak their minds about what's not working, making space for new things that might. As a result, we've removed some of our regular meetings altogether, or we've blown them up and put them back together in new ways. Just a single conversation like that can save us days over the course of a year.

This mentality gives everyone the confidence to air their ideas. We get things wrong, and not every idea is a path worth following, but we create a culture of healthy questioning.

KEEP IT SMALL – THE TWO PIZZA RULE

Amazon's Jeff Bezos uses the 'two pizza rule' to define the maximum number of people that should be in a meeting, or indeed a team. The rule is simple. Never hold a meeting where you couldn't feed all of the participants with two pizzas. As a rough rule, any meeting with more than around six people starts to lose some efficiency. This is particularly important for decision-making meetings (although of course where the goal is more about blanket communication across a whole organisation, then you'll either need to break this rule, order some more pizzas, or occasionally just send an email instead).

For many of the organisations we work with, the culture is to invite everyone that might have a connection to the work being discussed to a meeting, no matter how small that connection. It's rare that a lot of thought is put into how many people are actually needed. Changing that culture can be tough. Creating a culture where a meeting invite is rare, where meetings are small and focused rather than large and disorganised, is a key way that many businesses could easily up their game. Seeking the right balance between the yin of inclusion and the yang of ruthless attendance is the ultimate goal.

STALE

There's an African proverb that says 'even the best dancers get tired'. The same is true for regular gatherings. A common cycle is for an employee to decide 'we need a regular meeting', perhaps to share information, ensure everyone is communicating, or to fix a common set of problems. When the meeting starts up, it feels innovative, fresh and new. Perhaps it fixes some of those problems and makes an impact. But as time goes on, it becomes boring. You've heard the same things before. It starts to feel like you're all going through the motions. It feels stale.

Usually what then happens, someone invents a new format or tries something different within the meeting. And often, one of the more long-serving colleagues pipes up to tell everyone that this exact cycle, of replacing a shorter meeting with a longer one, or vice versa, is exactly what happened eight years ago. Sometimes these formats are just going around in a cyclical loop.

There's actually nothing wrong with this. It's a natural cycle. Think of it like how the seasons of the year affect a tree. If you're the person who first planted the tree, you don't need to take it personally when the leaves fall off. In the same way, it's not a direct criticism of the meeting organiser, but you can look out for when meetings start to go stale and try to bring about something better. You can encourage people to identify early on when things might need to change, promoting an engaged environment.

CULTURE OF GOOD REPORTING = MINIMALIST MEETINGS CULTURE

Communication in a team is about quality not quantity. It's easy to confuse a hundred Slack channels, everyone sending reply-all emails all the time, or a daily Zoom call with good communication, but in truth, all you have is a lot of noise. In any individual role, team or organisation, you should be able to pinpoint the one, two, or three key metrics – those measurements that really make a difference and indicate that performance is on track. Figuring out how you share this data in particular can make a huge difference to the number of peripheral meetings being organised. A good rule of thumb here is 'visual and often'. Put these key metrics on a whiteboard that everyone gathers around each morning, or have them pride of place on the dashboard of whatever the key software your team is using (whether that's a CRM, your finance app or a task-based app) or have them clearly laid out in a weekly report that everyone receives. This 'anchoring' to the core data will help maintain focus and avoid a lot of unnecessary 'mission drift' conversation. Creating this culture of good reporting requires yang energy. It helps to have clarity around who the decision-makers are, who needs to receive certain information and what the purpose behind each meeting and metric is.

While it may seem counter-intuitive, we often find companies that cut down on email also waste less time in meetings. This is because they've taken time and care to establish the ground rules around communication.

THE SEED OF YIN IN YANG

The energy of yang can be destructive. Strategies like 'blowing up' the norm or ruthless non-attendance of meetings are unlikely to make sense politically in an organisation or immediately win you favours. We are all so hard-wired from our time in education to see any deviation from the standard ways of operating as risky, mischievous or even wrong. So when we're in the middle of fiery action, it's worth having one eye on the yin, and one ear out to listen – even when we're heads down and avoiding meetings. It means being tactful, sensitive and thoughtful about how best to 'sell' changes in culture to your team. And it means recognising that too much of the abrasive yang – without any of the calming and cooler energy of yin – is unlikely to have a positive result.

So we end this section, and this chapter, with a reminder of where we started: by saying that it's not about being one way or the other, it's about balance. Yes, we have focused more heavily on the yang qualities in this chapter, but that's because a great deal of the practical stuff in the next chapters veers more to the yin side. The key is recognising that both need their opposite to function properly.

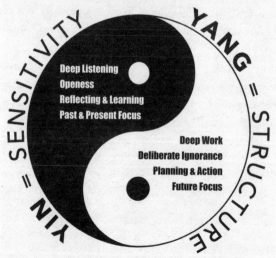

EXERCISE: ARE YOU MORE YIN OR YANG?

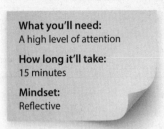

What you'll need:
A high level of attention

How long it'll take:
15 minutes

Mindset:
Reflective

Do you naturally identify with the energy of yin or yang in your work? Use the table of qualities below to check out if you are more yin, yang or have a good balance.

Yin	Yang
Collaborative	Autonomous
Listens deeply	Prone to interrupt or not always pay full attention
Tends to overrun	Sticks to the time allocated
Consensus-building	Target-focused
Focused on thoughts, lessons and people	Action-focused

Now ask yourself the following questions:

▶ Would you say that the culture of your organisation means you spend too much time in meetings and need more of the fiery, occasionally ruthless yang energy, to make way for the deep work?

▶ When you do meet, is it generally shallow waffle, or deep listening that seeks to understand the people and problems that you're dealing with?

▶ What can you do to get yin and yang more in balance when it comes to meetings?

Once you have identified if your meetings are more yin or yang, consider if you need more of the opposing force. Think about what you could do differently in your upcoming meetings to achieve a better balance.

YOU WILL KNOW THAT YOU ARE FIXING MEETINGS WHEN:

▶ You bring a good balance of yin and yang to meetings that you attend.

▶ Meetings you organise involve only the people that are needed and are shorter than before.

▶ You can look back at the previous weeks and reflect that your meetings were mostly a productive use of your energy and attention.

3.
BEFORE THE MEETING

HANDLE WITH CARE: THE 40-20-40 CONTINUUM

We've looked at how we need to change our approach to meetings generally, to ensure that we promote deep listening and collaboration. The next three chapters are more practical, focusing on the three most important aspects of meetings: before, during and after.

We've been inspired over the years by working with some great facilitators (people who artfully manage meetings and other group interactions to reach a common purpose). The most notable is Martin Farrell, who has been part of the Think Productive team as well as a professional facilitator, working with organisations like the UN, the British Council and NATO. It's a joy to watch him work, because it feels like he's doing magic. It's why we called him our 'meetings magician'. He has a knack for getting people talking constructively about the difficult stuff and an ability to lead people towards constructive outcomes. In Martin's words, each organisation 'hands over the car keys' and trusts him to steer things in the right direction – perhaps for an afternoon, for a day, or for a conference lasting several days.

Martin contributed to the book *Meeting Together*, along with Lois Graessle and George Gawlinski, and this book introduced us to a principle that we've followed ever since: The 40-20-40 Continuum.

The 40-20-40 Continuum describes how we should direct our energy and attention in relation to each meeting:

▶ 40% on the preparation for the meeting

▶ 20% on the meeting itself

▶ 40% on the productive follow-through

Most people's focus tends to be almost 100% on the meeting itself, with little regard for either the preparation and design of the meeting, or the follow-through to make everything happen. This often leads to long-winded meetings that produce little results. Perhaps you already go to a good number of those, which is why you picked up this book?

While it's more obvious to see where the attention is needed outside of the meeting if you're the organiser, the chances are that even as a participant there's reading and preparation to do beforehand if you value the time you're investing into your participation, and there's follow-through in terms of actions or further thinking afterwards.

In each of the following three chapters you'll find all the practical tips and tricks to make your meetings magical and productive places. Before we dive in though, a couple of observations about the implications of 40-20-40:

1. If you're in back-to-back meetings on Monday, the rest of your week should be meeting-free!

   Think about it. If one full day out of five has been filled with meetings, that's already 20% of your work week taken up. For the rest of the week, you need time to follow up on what was agreed in those meetings, as well as to plan and prepare for the meetings coming up next week. When we look at things in this way, suddenly all these ruthlessness tactics don't feel quite so naughty or unnecessary.

2. Focusing on the preparation and design of meetings is what creates the magic.

   Martin would often say to us that the real magic doesn't happen on the day, it happens in the preparation. It's in knowing the context of the participants, understanding their issues, having a discussion beforehand with some of the key people about the boundaries of what can be discussed, and so on. As you will see when we get to the next chapter, it's also about how you invite people enticingly and make your meeting stand out.

3. The productive follow-through needs to be part of the culture.

   Meetings can be cosy, with their cookies and chit-chat, but they also need to resolve in pushing people outside of their comfort zones, getting commitments on the big things that need to be done and getting buy-in from the right people. It's about designing the meeting and then steering it so that the expectations are clear, and everyone leaves with a firm idea of their next actions.

FAILING TO PREPARE ...

The quality of a meeting depends on the quality of its preparation. This chapter will help you practice preparedness in every aspect of your meetings – whether you're the organiser or a participant.

We'll start with a look at how to design meetings with the user in mind. We'll give you some practical ideas to implement and exercises to help you get started with planning your meetings. It's useful to know about this even if you aren't the meeting designer, as some of the ideas will help you to be a great participant too.

The next section is about formats – how to choose the best format from our menu of options, to make your meetings memorable and fit for purpose. As the meeting designer it's down to you to match the menu choice to the occasion.

We will finish off this chapter by taking a look at what you can do to prepare when you're not the meeting organiser – we call it steering from the back seat. We will introduce you to some ideas to help you influence the success of the meeting, and to boost the effectiveness of your attention before it even gets started.

Remember that your company's culture around meetings is likely to be very different to someone else's. While reading these chapters we encourage you to think about what will apply to your organisation. Many will feel that more agile types of meetings work better in smaller organisations, whereas for people working in a more regulated environment there might be more restrictions. For those in global companies or with remote teams, online meetings will be the norm. How do you get brave and push the boundaries? Think about what is most appropriate for you and your situation, but don't confuse appropriate with easy. If you think it's not appropriate, always question why, and challenge that assumption. Sometimes you will be right, but sometimes the answer might be to be brave and give it a try.

WHY THE 'FIRST 40' REALLY MATTERS

Let's face it, at one point or another we've all 'winged it', doing no prep and just rocking up to a meeting. This is probably quite common for meeting participants, but often the person chairing the meeting does it too. Chances are, you don't have the best meeting, you don't get the best results and you perhaps even feel embarrassed or forced to acknowledge that you haven't put the effort in. Hayley knows this feeling well. She once agreed to attend a meeting at a school where she is a governor. She had not prepared, and really should have. She thought that she was meeting with someone who was going to explain some of her responsibilities in relation to a specific aspect of funding. In fact, it was an external assessor who was there to make sure that the Board of Governors understood their responsibilities. This was hugely embarrassing for Hayley, who was then questioned about this aspect of funding and how the school was spending it. Getting caught out through a lack of preparation is beneath you and unprofessional. If you can't do the preparation, ask yourself if this meeting is worthy of your attention. If it is, it's also worthy of your preparation.

WHAT CAN YOU DO TODAY THAT PROVIDES A GIFT TO YOUR FUTURE SELF?

This is what the characteristic of preparedness is all about. Doing things today that will make tomorrow, and the days and weeks after, feel much easier. Often, you can do this with just a small investment of your energy and attention. If you start to apply this attitude to meetings, it can make a huge difference to your working life, making it run more smoothly. And who wouldn't want a bit of that?

> **• REMEMBER •**
>
> By asking what you can do today that will make your future meetings better, you set yourself up to make life easier in the future.

PROVOKING PLEASURE

User Experience Design (often referred to as UX design) is defined as 'the process of enhancing user satisfaction with a product by improving the usability, accessibility, and pleasure provided in the interaction with the product'.[1] It's described by John Amir-Abbassi of

Dropbox as 'an approach to design that takes the user into account'.[2] So here's a radical idea: what if meetings could give you as much pleasure, and work just as efficiently, as your favourite software or app? What if participants genuinely felt like their views and experience were taken into account? There's plenty we can learn from UX design to help make this happen, so here are what are commonly referred to as the '6 stages of UX design' and then some observations about how we can use these stages to design brilliant meetings.[3]

1. UNDERSTAND USERS AND ORGANISATIONS

UX designers work hard to understand the basic intersection between the users and the brand or mission of the company. 'Who should we aim this at?', 'What are our brand's values and ambitions?', 'What problem are we trying to solve?' These are more philosophical questions than the ones we're used to writing on a meeting agenda, but we'll talk in the next section about why defining a meeting's purpose is even more important than writing the agenda. Think about who should be at your meeting and how they best contribute. Are they quiet people or will they have lots to say? What problems are they trying to solve in their work? What do they really care about (no one cares about meetings per se!)?

2. RESEARCH

In software or web design, it's important to research and understand your potential users and test your assumptions. A common approach is to develop 'avatars' or 'buyer personas' that describe people of certain demographics, or in certain situations, trying to solve specific problems. You can then use questionnaires or other market research to test that the problem is real and the solution is popular. A shortcut here is to speak to 3–5 people that fit the profile of your 'ideal user'. This is also a very useful thing to do before sending out invites to a meeting. By talking to some of the potential attendees, it will help you clarify the purpose of the meeting, and you'll also likely get some feedback about the appetite for the meeting. Is this meeting helping other people to solve their problems too, or are you just asking them to give up their time to help you solve yours? What else could or should be on the agenda? By having very quick conversations like this with a small number of people, you'll get bonus information that will help the preparation and performance of the meeting.

3. ANALYSE

With these conversations and ideas fresh in your mind, you can start to make decisions about the kind of meeting you need – or whether, of course, there are better ways to accomplish the task that aren't so costly. Can you make it shorter? Should you broaden the scope based on what your manager said? Are there people who don't need to be there, but need to be informed that it's taking place? How can you maximise the time you'll have together, so that it's as useful as possible?

4. DESIGN

In software UX, the design phase is where you sketch out 'wireframes' or make very lo-fi prototypes of what you're hoping to build. You might create site-maps and start to visualise what the finished product might look like. We should take similar approaches to meetings! Write out an agenda that includes a purpose statement. Sketch in your mind how some of the major discussions might play out. Give some thought to potential conflicts, which parts of the meeting might drag, how best to present information and how to make sure the meeting is as user-friendly as possible. We'll look at these things in more detail later in this chapter.

5. LAUNCH

It's the big one. The launch! The meeting itself. Do you notice how this step of the process is the fifth of six? That's how you make meetings smooth, productive and user-friendly.

6. ANALYSE (AGAIN)

The final phase in UX design is about learning from the launch and initial user feedback. Launch, test, improve. The cycle continues. This is an often-neglected but radical idea when it comes to meetings. There are good reasons why people hosting meetings don't normally spend much time evaluating them. Asking for feedback from the group in the room feels risky – it exposes you to potential criticism. Doing it after the event, via a SurveyMonkey or email survey, can feel like extra work that you're putting on the participants. But in our experience, creating the culture of psychological safety where everyone can analyse the effectiveness of collaboration is one of the most rewarding and productive things any team can do.

So what?

What can we take from this as we think about meetings? Well, have you noticed how often the first action around a meeting seems to be someone booking a meeting room and sending you a meeting invite? So much of the preliminary thinking that a UX designer would employ seems absent from corporate meeting culture. It's no wonder meetings don't feel like pleasurable experiences (and in many cases, that's a massive understatement).

Using a more considered approach, we can begin to design meeting experiences that are more enjoyable, more productive, and that respect the other time commitments of colleagues.

THE 4 PS: PURPOSE. PLAN. PROTOCOLS. PEOPLE

As the meeting organiser or 'designer', you can use the 4 Ps to make great meetings happen: Purpose, Plan, Protocols and People. This is a nice framework to use for planning meetings in advance, but also useful if you ever end up in an emergency or impromptu meeting and are scrabbling around for a structure – agreeing the basics around the 4 Ps is a productive place to start, as they are the building blocks of a successful meeting. Getting one of them wrong can lead to long-winded meetings that don't have a conclusion or result in action, and that waste the participants' valuable attention. The kind that you are already used to, perhaps.

4
- PURPOSE
- PLAN
- PROTOCOL
- PEOPLE

▶ **Purpose:** The purpose will help define who attends the meeting, what will be said and how you'll know that the meeting has achieved its goal. As a meeting organiser, you can help people by clearly communicating to others the purpose of your meeting. We want you to do this when you first invite them. The meeting doesn't have to finish at the agreed end time. It should ideally finish before then, and never afterwards. If your purpose is clear, it will be obvious when the meeting is done.

▶ **Plan:** The plan is about letting people know how your meeting will run. Have you ever been to a meeting not knowing when it finishes, or when or if there will be a break? It sets you up with a sense of uncertainty about how things are going to work out. If you are organising the meeting, either in person or online, let participants know the start and end times beforehand, as well as times of breaks or refreshments, as it will help people to manage their attention throughout the discussion.

▶ **Protocols:** The protocols are often subtler things that can be done to help engage people and make sure the discussion runs smoothly. What will the ground rules be? These might include confidentiality of the discussion, guidelines around how mobile phones and laptops are used in the meeting, or practices such as having just one person speaking at a time. For online meetings, protocols are likely to include guidelines for how people ask questions, how to get the attention of the chair, or how participants can share views.

▶ **People:** It's about getting the right people there. This is a delicate balance of quality over quantity – you don't want too many, you don't want too few. Having the right people attending the meeting will make all the difference, and if you don't have that, the other stuff becomes obsolete.

So, let's put this into practice. Let's think now about how you can use the 4 Ps to maximise success in your own meeting. Let's start with Purpose.

> 'You have a meeting to make a decision, not to decide on the question.' – Bill Gates

KNOW YOUR PURPOSE

We firmly believe that all meetings should have a purpose statement: a sentence or two that states in clear terms exactly why you are meeting and what the meeting is trying to achieve.

Regular meetings, such as team meetings, should have a different purpose each time. Although the broader purpose might be the same, the content of your discussion should change. Otherwise you would just be repeating yourself each time.

Sharing the purpose statement in advance means that everyone has the same understanding of what the meeting is about and what the end goal looks like.

Focusing on the purpose of the meeting can help everyone to understand their role and why you want them to be involved. You can use this to help steer the conversation, but it can also help people to decide if they want to attend or not. It's one of the things that makes a huge difference to our clients in our Fixing Meetings session. Often people who are planning to attend the same meeting will have a very different idea about what the purpose of that meeting is, meaning that it's unlikely the purpose will be met for them all.

EXAMPLE OF A BOARD MEETING PURPOSE STATEMENT:

By the end of the meeting, the board will have:

▶ Noted the quarterly results and confirmed our intentions for investment

▶ Scrutinised and agreed the proposed strategic plan for next year

▶ Discussed the upcoming board recruitment

▶ Identified any new strategic issues or opportunities to be taken forward by the executive team

EXAMPLE OF A REGULAR TEAM MEETING PURPOSE STATEMENT:

By the end of the meeting we will have:

▶ Discussed our work and plans for the next week

▶ Identified any problems or bottlenecks

▶ Decided on our big priorities for next months' campaign

EXAMPLE OF A ONE-OFF OPERATIONAL MEETING PURPOSE STATEMENT:

By the end of this meeting, we will have:

▶ Agreed the scope of the problem

▶ Discussed our barriers to solving it

▶ Confirmed the actions that each of us are taking over the next 1/2/3 weeks to overcome these barriers

---

• REMEMBER •

Every meeting should have a purpose statement. Start with: 'By the end of this meeting we will have ...'. Verbs to use:

- Decided/Agreed
- Discussed
- Resolved
- Learned
- Confirmed
- Noted/Received
- Identified

EXERCISE: PURPOSE STATEMENT

What you'll need:
Somewhere to take notes, and your
calendar so you can see your upcoming
meetings

How long it'll take:
Depends on how many meetings you
have! Pick two to get started and this will
take 10–15 minutes

Mindset:
Preparedness

Select a meeting that you have identified as being an excellent
use of your attention in the next week (it doesn't matter if you
are responsible for the meeting, or if you are going along as an
attendee). Write your purpose statement:

PLAN

Now that you have clarity on your purpose, let's turn our focus to how you plan the meeting. All the planning we do here is to make sure your meeting has the building blocks in place to achieve that purpose.

AGENDA

One of the most common tools for meetings is an agenda: a list of the topics that will be discussed in your meeting. Without an agenda, it is a lot harder for attendees to prepare. Research in 2017 claimed that 63% of meetings in America were conducted without a pre-planned agenda. Even more will have been lacking a purpose statement.[4]

Detail within an agenda is important. A marketeer doesn't want to come to a meeting with an agenda item that just says 'Marketing'. To help them decide whether or not they should attend, and to best prepare for your meeting, provide more detail.

Hayley used to manage an organisation that promoted and supported volunteering. A partner organisation that she regularly met with would often add 'Volunteering' to the agenda of their meeting. This didn't help her to prepare – she had a team of people who all worked on different areas of volunteering. So Hayley would pick up the phone and ask what would be covered in the agenda item. When she didn't do this, she would often find that during the meeting people wanted data that she didn't have to hand. Hayley's prep would include understanding what people wanted to know, then finding the data, understanding it, and getting up to speed with progress on this work area. Understanding what someone wanted to achieve from a specific agenda item helped her decide if it should be her attending the meeting or someone else within her team.

We have already explained the importance of having an overall purpose statement for the meeting. Each agenda item should then have its own purpose outlined – what people could do to prepare, how long each item will take, and who is responsible for that item. If you are the meeting organiser, we encourage you to let people know if you want them to lead on a specific item, or if they need to come prepared to talk about specific issues. It's important to be clear about expectations to ensure that your participants are as prepared as possible.

Agenda template

Meeting name, date, and start and finish time
For example:

Think Productive Conference 2021
21st April 10.10–10.50

Purpose of meeting
A brief overview of the meeting's purpose, and then a list of who is invited, including a sentence or two to explain what they are being asked to contribute. (If someone from a team [for example marketing] is required to give their input, this can be made clear here and then the team can decide who is best placed to attend.)

For example:
To agree content for Think Productive's annual conference. To provide the marketing team with the information they need to provide a draft marketing plan. This is our first annual conference and we want it to run smoothly. By the end of the meeting we will have defined what we need to do to make this happen.

Janet: We will need your involvement in planning how to pro-
           mote the conference. This will primarily be work for your
           team going forwards so attendance from you or a deci-
           sion maker in your team is essential.

Simon: We would like you to join our meeting because you have
           a good overview of our clients and what they are looking
           for from this event. Please come to the meeting prepared
           to share these insights in agenda item two.

Raj: As we plan the conference, your knowledge of the venue
           would be a real asset to these discussions. It would be
           really helpful if you could capture actions from the meet-
           ing to share on Slack after the meeting as agreed on
           Friday.

Mike: You have expressed interest in being involved in planning
           the conference, so we are inviting you to attend if that is
           of interest and you have the capacity to take actions on
           this.

Ilona: Leading on operational delivery of the conference.
(Chair)   Please come to the meeting with a clear idea of the
           number of delegates needed to break even.

Agenda item	Purpose (e.g. to decide, for info, to generate ideas etc.)	What can people do to prepare?	Person responsible	Time allocated to this item
		Everyone needs to read the update attached to the meeting invite. This two-page doc is mainly bullet points updating on progress since last meeting, including sponsorship, venue and confirmed speakers.		
1. Welcome and introductions	Introductions and allocate a timekeeper		Ilona	3 mins
2. Client insights	To define what clients are currently looking for from the conference	Discussions with clients, asking what they would find most useful?	Raj	15 mins
3. Marketing strategy	To define what the marketing team need to know to come up with a good marketing plan	Consider who the event is aimed at, what needs does the event meet for them? Ilona to provide clarity on minimum and maximum numbers attending	Emma	15 mins
4. Review of meeting	To ask if we achieved our purpose, whether we had the right people attending and what we can do to improve
Everyone to clarify their next actions		Ilona	7 mins

You can download a template at thinkproductive.com/meetingresources

EXERCISE: AN AGENDA THAT GIVES CLARITY

What you'll need:
The purpose statement(s) from the previous
exercise, and if it's a recurring meeting,
perhaps find the agenda or minutes from the
last time it took place

How long it'll take:
10–15 minutes

Mindset:
Preparedness

Work out what steps you need to take to achieve your meeting's
purpose. Create an agenda that helps you towards your goal. Use
the template. Remember to use sentences, not key words, for your
agenda. Give clarity to each agenda item. Include what you would
like people to do, to help them prepare for this discussion. This will
include instructions for specific individuals if their role in relation to
that agenda item is different to other attendees. Note: don't worry
too much about timings at this point – we'll come on to that shortly.

> **• REMEMBER •**
>
> The 4 Ps helps you set a framework for a successful meeting.
> Purpose, Plan, Protocols and People.

WHAT'S THE STORY?

What about if you know roughly what needs to be discussed, but don't have a clear idea of what order to take things in? It can sometimes be helpful to think about the 'narrative arc' of a meeting. What's the journey that you're hoping to embark upon? Here are three simple formulas that we've used over the years.

Beginning, middle and end

So many classic pieces of fiction follow a three-act formula: beginning, middle and end. The beginning is usually about establishing a situation and a problem, the middle contains the struggle and conflict, and the end is the resolution. This can be as useful for a mundane accounts meeting as it is for Hollywood scriptwriters. Start with identifying the problem and context; the middle is about ideas, solutions and routes through the situation; the end is about resolutions, actions and next steps.

Rudyard Kipling's 'Six Honest Serving-Men'

Staying with the literary theme, Rudyard Kipling's famous poem begins 'I keep six honest serving-men. (They taught me all I knew); Their names are What and Why and When, And How and Where and Who.'

Great meetings ask great questions. If you're planning a new product, or looking to fully interrogate an idea, one helpful structure we have used is to run through each of these questions in turn.

GROW model

Borrowed from coaching, the GROW model is also a useful way to structure a journey through a meeting. The model has the following four stages:

▶ **Goal:** A clearly defined end point that the person or team wants to get to.

▶ **Reality:** The current situation, challenges and issues.

▶ **Options:** What are the different ways to reach the goal?

▶ **Way Forward:** Picking the right options and turning them into actions!

There are of course many other ways to tell stories too, but we find that giving some structure to the discussion can help provide a focus that saves time and keeps things on track.

WHAT TIME?

Starting and finishing meetings on the hour is what most people do, so how about trying something else? A team we worked with decided that meetings weren't going to start before ten past the hour and had to be finished before ten to the hour. This would allow people time to move from one meeting to the next, to digest what had taken place, and perhaps get a drink or visit the bathroom. It meant the meetings were shorter too.

LATE COMERS

You've received an agenda with a meeting's start time, but you arrive a few minutes late and it's already started – you're the last one in. If you are anything like us, you feel a bit bad, slide into the meeting and try to understand what is going on as quickly as possible.

What happens next time you are planning to get to that meeting? Now that you know the meeting starts on time, chances are you make the extra effort to be there on time. Where the culture is to start late, start times just get later and later.

For online meetings, always plan to log in at least five minutes early, and allow more time if you are the host. This avoids the rushing around, realising that the tool you are using needs to install an update or your microphone isn't working. Allow a few minutes for everyone to log in at the start in your agenda, and explain that if everyone is logged in early the meeting will get started.

TWO-MINUTE ACTIONS

What happens to most of us when we go back to our desks after a meeting? Perhaps we procrastinate a bit, check in with emails, make a cup of tea. Often colleagues will see that you are back and ask you questions about the email they have just sent that you haven't read yet. Sound familiar?

How about you add ten minutes to the end of the meeting agenda for all attendees to complete any quick two-minute actions? As David Allen suggests in his book *Getting Things Done*, things that take two minutes shouldn't make it to your to-do list, they should just be done straight away. Adding time into the agenda for people to do any quick two-minute actions, or capture and perhaps organise bigger tasks (for those of you used to the Ninja way of working, this is the first two stages of CORD) could mean that more gets done and people leave the meeting having already made a start on their actions. This might require some use of technology to make quick calls or send emails after the meeting, so you'd need to give some thought to how devices are managed during the meeting, given that you are permitting them to be in the room.

These extra ten minutes provide your meeting attendees with a bit of stealth and camouflage – a space in which they can do some work (or at the very least, capture clear actions for later) without being interrupted. You can use this for online meetings too by suggesting everyone stays logged in.

TICK. TOCK.

Have you gone to a meeting that you made a real effort to be on time for, only to find that everyone was just chatting about their weekend, the kids, the awful film they saw the night before, and anything else not related to the topic of the meeting? For many people, meetings are about coming together socially with colleagues, and the chatting before and after is an opportunity to build rapport, to check in with each other and get to know one another better. For others, they just want to get on with the meeting because they have a busy day.

Wouldn't it be better if the meeting organiser sent an email like this one?

> Hi Graham
>
> For the finance meeting on Friday, the room is booked for 2pm.
>
> There will be tea, coffee and snacks available. If anyone wants to have an informal catch up, please join us at 2pm for a chat. The first agenda item will begin at 2.22pm, and you are welcome to just join us then if you prefer to come along only for the business part of the meeting.
>
> See you Friday (agenda and purpose statement are attached).
>
> Best wishes,
> Hayley

That would allow people a choice about how they wanted to use their time.

Jeff Bezos of Amazon has shared one of his meetings practices. He requires that a six-page memo be given to attendees at the start of each meeting, providing background information and detailing the topics to be covered.[5] He then allocates time at the start of each meeting for everyone to read the memo. He is quoted as saying: 'If we don't, the executives, like high school kids, will try to bluff their way through a meeting.'

Requiring people to do this together might not work for everyone, for a variety of reasons. People's reading times differ, it could make some feel unprepared as they enter a meeting, or some simply won't have this extra time in their day. An alternative would be to give succinct information to participants beforehand, so they can plan and prepare at their own pace. Much like offering some extra time in the room for a social purpose, you could offer the option for people to come before the meeting to prepare, or arrive at a later time if they have prepared in their own time.

EXERCISE: TIMING

What you'll need:
Agenda from the previous exercise

How long it'll take:
5 minutes

Mindset:
Ruthlessness and Agility

Allocate time to each agenda item. Think about what would be a good time for your meeting to start and end. Include any preparation, logging in, or socialising time where you feel it would be helpful.

WHAT'S THE PROBLEM?

Susan Cain (an expert on introverts) tells us that about half of the population are introverts, and are likely to do their best thinking away from the meeting. Providing more information on what will be tackled in a meeting – the meat of the problem you are looking to overcome – will help everyone to understand the issues and think about their ideas before they come together.[6] This information is different to the purpose statement and agenda.

An example purpose statement might be: 'We will make decisions about how to improve internal communication.' The agenda might then include detail on how this will be approached such as brainstorming ideas, then evaluating them, then deciding what ideas to explore and pilot, followed by discussion about how success will be evaluated. What all of this is lacking is some clarity on what the issue is, how it has come about and who wants to improve it and why. This can all be done before the meeting, via presentation slides or bullet points, or by recording a brief outline of the issue by video or audio. Sharing it before the meeting allows people to think about the problem that the meeting is trying to solve, and perhaps seek to better understand it.

> • REMEMBER •
>
> Provide as much information before the meeting as possible, so you use your time together to create rather than update.

AOB: ANY OLD BALONEY?

AOB stands for 'Any Other Business', and is used a lot in UK organisations to end meetings. It's a time for participants to raise anything that hasn't been mentioned during the course of the meeting that they feel should be included in the discussion.

When planning what will and won't make it onto your agenda, consider if AOB is your friend or foe. We think that there tend to be two types of responses to AOB from participants. One is: great, this meeting is almost over. The other is: great, now I get to mention all the things that I think should have been on the agenda.

We have attended board meetings where the meeting organiser got rid of AOB altogether. A few weeks before the meeting, there would be an email reminding people about the meeting and asking if anything needed to be added to the agenda. This meant that the meeting ran to time and everyone's points were included. There are of course times when this might not work – an urgent issue could arise that needs discussion. In this situation, the issue could be added to the agenda at the start of the meeting, allowing people to agree to what gets less time so that this point can be discussed.

Another option is replacing AOB with an agenda point at the start of a meeting, called 'Any updates' or 'Matters arising' – a chance for people to provide an update on things that affect the agenda because something has changed since it was put together. It needs to be relevant to the purpose of the meeting.

WIGGLE IT!

When planning the agenda or chairing the meeting, leaving a little wiggle room can really help you, but there is a balance to strike. Too much wiggle room and your meeting will drag, losing people's attention. Not enough wiggle room, and you miss the opportunity to explore things that you hadn't anticipated being raised, or to allow people time to think more clearly. If your meeting is timetabled for 45 minutes, for example, can you allow about seven minutes of wiggle room in your agenda?

If some items take less time than planned, it can be tempting to try and 'pad' the next item to 'get back onto time', but of course if you stay ahead of your schedule, you now have this time to give as a gift back to people at the end. If you can do this every time, you and your meetings will be well regarded.

PREDICTING THE ODDLY PREDICTABLE

There may be times where you know in advance what the sticking points in a meeting are likely to be. Try to look for these before you get together and develop some strategies for overcoming them. Edward De Bono's Thinking Hats tool can come in handy here (see p. 150). There may be other times where a sticking point comes as a complete surprise.

We spoke to Martin Farrell (an expert facilitator) about tensions in meetings, using a situation we'd experienced in a workshop as an example. There were two people in a group of about fourteen who disagreed with each other on every suggestion made about how they might change their use of email. The workshop was fast becoming a stage for them to play out their difference of opinion. Someone sat between them and said (while the two individuals carried on speaking), 'They always do this. Every single meeting.' Martin pointed out that in this situation, it probably didn't matter what the topic of conversation was about – these people were always likely to disagree. He suggested that if you have people whose reactions can be anticipated in this way, you could ask them to discuss the issue and share their concerns together before the meeting so that others don't have to listen to them doing this. Some sort of mediation might be more beneficial in the long term. Healthy debate is to be encouraged, but personal differences and disagreements are less useful.

WHEN YOU KNOW IT'S COMING ...

Are there conversations to be had more informally before the meeting? Especially for board meetings and team meetings, it can be worth lobbying people in advance to find out their views, to make your case, or to encourage some more critical thinking. Part of your planning for the meeting might include thinking about how your views and ideas fit with those of others. Consider where support and objections might come from and make overcoming these objections part of your pre-meeting preparation. Think about how you can frame your ideas and contributions so that they will appeal to others. Once you are in the meeting, it's important to listen to the ideas of others and be willing to change your views based on discussion. Preparing and ordering your thinking will help with this.

MULTITASKING

Have you ever made a mistake while multitasking? We all have. One of Graham's first jobs was as the CEO of a small charity. He'd organised an all-day board meeting and was then going straight to the airport for a holiday he'd planned with his girlfriend. Because his attention was on the board meeting, they were cutting it fine, crossing London to get to Heathrow airport just in time. The only problem was that the flight was leaving from Gatwick, an hour or so back in the other direction. Epic fail. Trying to do two things at once, even simple things, can lead to mistakes.

In our fast-paced culture there is an expectation that we should be able to do more than one thing at a time. This is how we end up with statistics that say things like 92% of people in a meeting are multitasking.[7] What that actually means in practice is that almost everyone spends some time in a meeting doing something else. In fact, less than 2% of the population can multitask with any level of effectiveness.[8] We want people to be engaged in our meetings, so that they don't feel the need to multitask.

What to do before your meeting to avoid multitasking:
▶ Don't use your meeting time to present information to people. Do this beforehand. This information could be in written form, or you could deliver your presentation in front of a camera if you prefer to verbalise, or send it as a voice memo. Tools like

Screencast allow you to record your screen and audio input if you have data or images that you would like to share.

▶ Make sure that when you plan your agenda and timings, the pace will be fast enough to keep people focused on the topic.

▶ Make clear in your invites what people will be expected to do during the meeting.

▶ Give people a role, especially if you know from experience that they are often daydreaming or working on something else.

▶ Make it clear that for online meetings, people will be expected to have their camera on.

LOCATION, LOCATION, LOCATION

The room a meeting takes place in, and its layout, can speak volumes about how much you value the meeting and the ideas of those assembled. As a charity CEO, Hayley held an AGM every year, with varying numbers of attendees. AGM meetings are known for being optional and dull, so there isn't always a great incentive for people to be there. However, one year the venue was the British Museum, and attendance was far greater than previous years. People were interested in the venue; it felt important, interesting and out of the ordinary.

There might be times when meeting off-site can be a great advantage. Some feedback we received about one of our courses recently was that the client would have found it easier to concentrate on learning, and think more clearly, if they had not been in their regular office space. Sometimes taking people away from their usual surroundings can help them think in a different way. What spaces can you access, or how can you influence the space you do have to make it feel different? What can you do to make people feel more comfortable?

Shabby spaces

We don't all get to hold our meetings in the British Museum. Think about the spaces you have available. How can you use those spaces to show people that they matter? Some of you might have access to nice plush meeting rooms with comfy seats, breakout areas with sofas, or specially designed rooms with whiteboard walls and bean bags. Some of the spaces you have to work with might be less inviting, but you can still make small changes to demonstrate that the people attending are valued. Providing refreshments, setting up the room beforehand, or welcoming people as they arrive are all important ways to show your appreciation.

> • REMEMBER •
>
> You can communicate to people that they matter, regardless of the space you have available.

Online spaces

Let's think about how you can show people that they matter when the space is a virtual one. Making new people feel welcome is important to any meeting. You can do this in a virtual meeting by making sure anyone new to the meeting is teamed up with someone who knows how to use the technology and can assist them.

According to Doodle's 'The State of Meeting Report', 76% of people prefer face-to-face meetings, where picking up on social cues and body language is much easier.[9] Making your online meetings as much like face-to-face *'The environment should say "you matter"' – Nancy Kline* interaction as possible is therefore likely to improve the quality of your meeting. This can be done to a certain extent by asking everyone to have their cameras turned on. It is also important to think about your surroundings in an online meeting, so that you are comfortable and have everything you need, but that the background or setting isn't a distraction for others taking part.

You can still show participants that they matter, even if you're not meeting in person. Penny Pullan, in her book about virtual leadership, suggests sending participants a small gift such as a tea bag to make themselves a drink before the meeting, or a small pack of cookies. It doesn't have to be big, or expensive. It just shows that they matter and that you are thinking about them.

The little things are the big things

When we meet every six months as UK Productivity Ninjas, there is always a printed copy of the agenda available and anything else we might need for the meeting. Even though we all know each other well, we often arrive to find little gift bags, or surprises – as well as our favourite types of tea bags. On an occasion when Graham was unavoidably delayed, he arrived to find that although we had to start without him, there was a cup of tea waiting for him – a simple but lovely gesture showing that he was valued.

Think about where you meet, and how you lay out the room to say 'you matter'. At the very least this should be providing a glass of water for everyone, but you'd be surprised at how often this doesn't happen. If your meeting is happening off-site, these arrangements often need to be made in advance and so require particular attention (the checklist at the end of this chapter should help).

If your meeting is online, this doesn't mean that the little things should be neglected. If you'd usually distribute prizes or gifts at an in-person meeting, send them in advance so that people can open them during the meeting (or in one of the breaks).

The power of ... where you put the chairs

While this might sound a bit basic, looking at the room layout can be useful, especially if you use the same space often. Think about how the space will be seen by someone new – does it look inviting? What can you do to your meeting rooms to make them more welcoming, inspire creative thinking, or just be nicer environments to spend time in?

A theatre-style layout tends to suggest that people are about to be entertained, or perhaps lectured to. It doesn't suggest collaboration or that contribution will be encouraged. However, several tables with chairs around them suggests that participants will be more involved and that there will be informal discussions.

For some meetings, particularly ones with emotive content among a small group of people, a walking conversation could be better. Talking to someone while doing something practical, or being side by side rather than facing each other can make covering a tough subject easier. Do be aware of where you are and who else might be around – don't use this for conversations that require a confidential space.

EXERCISE: THE USUAL ROOM = THE USUAL RESULTS?

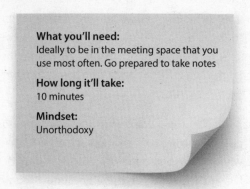

What you'll need:
Ideally to be in the meeting space that you use most often. Go prepared to take notes

How long it'll take:
10 minutes

Mindset:
Unorthodoxy

Try to look around the space with fresh eyes. Ask yourself:

▶ How might someone new joining the team view this space? What about it is inviting?

▶ What is not inviting? Can you change this?

Then ask yourself:

▶ What can you do in this space to show people that you value them and their attendance?

▶ What can you do to improve the space, or change how it is used?

PROTOCOLS

Protocols govern some of the more practical aspects of how a meeting is run. They ensure that everyone has a shared understanding of how their time together will work and can help to manage expectations. There can be protocols for things like how devices are used in meetings, how and when breaks will happen and for the allocation of roles such as timekeeper and note-taker. Protocols are likely to be even more necessary for online meetings.

LEFT TO THEIR OWN DEVICES?

Mobile technology is still relatively new, but it has crept up on us to the point where its use is rarely questioned. We both remember a time when mobile phones didn't exist, but they have quickly become an integral part of our lives – we are no more likely to leave home without them than without our shoes. It is definitely a good idea to set some intentions around phone use in meetings. Not to be luddites, or create rules that treat people like kids, but so that we can show respect for each other's contributions and offer our full concentration, making our time together more effective.

When we talk to people in our workshops about minimising the use of technology in face-to-face meetings, they can get very defensive. Imagine we told you right now that you need to put your phone in another room for the next two hours – you might feel a pang of resistance even just reading those words. There are several reasons for this. Firstly, we are asking people to change their behaviour, which no one likes to do. Secondly, there's an assumption in the request that their phones would disrupt the meeting or cause them to be less engaged (and no one likes being accused of something, not least before it's happened!). There may also be seemingly legitimate reasons for someone wanting to hold on to their phone, for example they may use their device to take notes.

Even with good intentions around bringing a phone to meetings, the problem is that these gadgets are designed to be addictive. Whenever we hear those pings, receive a new email, or see those red circles with numbers in them, our brains release dopamine. Dopamine is the brain's reward chemical and serves an important evolutionary purpose, but it can also be an irresistible distraction during meetings. Hence being a chair or meeting organiser who clarifies a healthy relationship with devices before (or at the start of) a meeting is one of the most important things we can do – but we also risk alienating people, particularly those who are less committed to the meeting or are already in a negative or stressed headspace as they arrive.

Six ways to ensure device-free meetings

▶ The phone box. Have a shoe box or similar in the room, and invite participants to put their phones in the box, either until the end of the meeting or until the break. Just the act of making this available will spark the conversation about what is and isn't appropriate meeting behaviour.

▶ Plant trees. Download the Forest app and work together to plant a tree in the real world. How does this work? You set a timer for the amount of time you want to be away from your phone. A tree begins to grow, but it dies if you start using your phone before the timer goes off. After growing a certain number of trees, you gain a coin which is used by the developers to donate money to a charity that plants trees.

▶ Raise awareness. Educate people on the science of why we are addicted to our phones. Then offer them a box for their phones during the meeting.

▶ Bribery. Chocolate biscuits for those willing to add their phone to the box.

▶ Change the environment. Move a meeting outside, or make it standing rather than sitting. Simple changes that take people outside of their usual meeting habits are often enough to disrupt their phone usage too.

▶ For online meetings, you can ask everyone to put their phone in a draw in a different room. Or, if you're using your phone for the online meeting, then make sure you've switched off any notifications that might pop up on the screen.

We are like moths drawn to the flame when it comes to our phones. You want to minimise the distractions so that you can maximise engagement.

For the people who want to take notes using their devices, get them to agree to turn off the Wi-Fi. Another alternative is to connect their phone to a shared screen or projector, so that everyone can see the notes as they are being typed up.

EXERCISE: PROTOCOLS

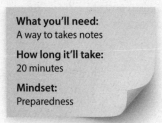

What you'll need:
A way to takes notes

How long it'll take:
20 minutes

Mindset:
Preparedness

What protocols are already in place for your meetings? Identify the ones that you find most useful.

What additional protocols would help increase engagement and manage expectations?

VIRTUAL PROTOCOLS

For online meetings, there are even more protocols to think about. Stuff goes wrong sometimes – that's life – and we want to run our online meetings in a way that is human enough to acknowledge this truth. By planning before the meeting, you can outline potential issues to people at the start of the discussion, letting them know what they should do if they have any technological problems. For example, during our webinars, someone at Think Productive Head Office will always be on hand to deal with any issues or questions at the start. This allows the person delivering the session to focus on doing just that.

IT'S ALL ABOUT THE PEOPLE

Have you ever been to a meeting, listened to your lovely colleagues or clients discussing stuff of importance, only to wonder what on earth you were invited for? It happens to us all. But now that you are practicing your ruthlessness, we hope that it is happening a lot less.

If you are running a meeting, be clear on why you are inviting each individual and make sure that they know this too. Imagine you receive a meeting invite that states why you are being asked to attend, and you're the only one in the organisation being asked for that specific reason. This makes it clear that your contribution is unique, and that people are going to be listening to what you have to say. What is expected of you is more obvious.

Which of these two meeting invites are you most likely to accept? Don't forget, you could still decline both.

Hi Jane

I am having a meeting on Monday to talk about training for our staff. Please come.

Thanks,
Chris

• • •

Hi Jane

I am getting together a number of organisations we have worked with in the past to explore how we could collaborate more closely in terms of our staff training. I am interested in looking at how we pool resources and expertise across our organisations. The purpose is to see if we can save money, and develop the skills of our people to a higher level.

I enjoyed talking with you at the networking event last week, and you mentioned that you were interested in accessing some coaching for your team and some training around meetings culture. Perhaps by pooling our resources we could work on this more effectively?

I have attached an agenda which outlines the areas I think could help us to achieve our purpose with this. Please come to the meeting with some ideas on your priorities in terms of staff training. I will ask everyone who attends to briefly share their thoughts on this.

I do hope that you can join us.

Thanks,
Chris

ROLES

It's often useful to assign roles for a meeting, the most obvious being that of a chairperson or 'chair', whose role it is to steer the discussion in the right direction. Chairing well requires many skills (which we will discuss in more detail later), so it's unrealistic to think the chair can cover all of the other necessary roles. Delegating certain other responsibilities, or asking for help, should not be seen as admitting weakness. Instead, it should be seen as an acknowledgment that being a chairperson is a complex role. Depending on the size and scope of a meeting, a number of other roles may be needed.

Timekeeper

Graham's timekeeping has never been the best (although, thankfully – and to many people, unbelievably – it's much better than before he wrote productivity books for a living). When chairing, Graham will often enlist the help of a timekeeper to give five-minute warnings or 'time checks' at different points. This serves a couple of useful functions. Firstly, it helps give Graham peace of mind that even if he gets carried away when trying to 'read the room' and focus more on the discussions, the meeting won't run over. Secondly, it can sometimes be a helpful dynamic for the participants to feel like the chair would happily hear all of their contributions, but isn't being 'allowed to' by the timekeeper. Good cop / bad cop.

Minute-taker

For formal meetings, particularly those that involve governance or where records of decisions might be useful for compliance, you're going to need someone to take minutes. Minutes can simply be a summary of the discussion, or can be more detailed to include individual contributions. Good practice is that the minutes are circulated to all participants, who then have a chance to confirm that they are an accurate reflection of the meeting.

Host

An often-overlooked role is that of the host. If you're chairing a meeting and want to keep your focus as much as possible on the substance, then having a designated host is a great idea. A host takes care of the meeting space and makes sure everyone is comfortable. They might formally welcome people as they arrive, take coats, provide drinks, give directions to the toilets, liaise with caterers and so on. Their role is ultimately to ensure that the participants and chair have everything they need for the meeting to run smoothly.

THE MORE THE MERRIER?

Invite too many people to a meeting and you could have an overwhelming amount of ideas, questions, opinions and personalities – and it may not be easy to reach a productive consensus. Invite not enough people and your board meeting isn't quorate, or if your team meeting doesn't involve the entire team then people may feel excluded. It's about getting the numbers right.

If you're not clear on who's needed and why, it's much easier to end up *over*-inviting people because you're scared of missing someone. We know that the larger the meeting, the harder it is to engage everyone effectively (and equally) and the more expensive the meeting is for your organisation. But did you also know that the number of 'channels of communication' rises exponentially as you add more people?[10]

The maths of over-inviting

When you have two people in a meeting, there's only a single channel of communication to think about. The simplicity of this means that both people can focus on the right thing: each other!

With three people, it starts to get a little more complicated. We now have three channels of communication, as each person is thinking about their work and ideas in relation to two others. Go beyond this and the growth is exponential. In fact, we can calculate it with the following formula:

$$n(n-1)/2,$$

(where n is the number of team members).

Using this formula, a meeting with four people would be 4 x 3 ÷ 2, resulting in six communication channels. That's more than the number of people in the meeting. Each person is conscious of how they relate to each of the other three.

With five people, (5 x 4 ÷ 2) a meeting suddenly has TEN separate communication channels. From there, you can see the rise:

Number of participants	Number of communication channels
3	3
4	6
5	10
6	15
7	21
8	28
10	45
15	105
20	190

Now, let's be honest. In a room full of twenty people, not each of those people will care (or need to care) about every single other participant, but there is still thinking and work involved in everything from learning names and roles, to working out whose toes you might be stepping on or the ways to get across your ideas while listening to the considerations of others (that may or may not be relevant!). This is all work that the organisation ultimately has to pay for.

3 PEOPLE

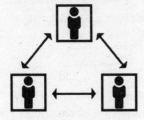

3 communication
channels

5 PEOPLE

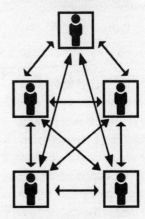

10 communication
channels

8 PEOPLE

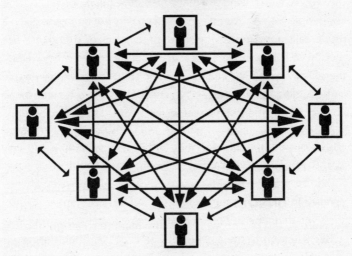

28 communication
channels

So every time you're sitting at your desk, tempted to add some more names to that meeting invite, remember the downside of too many communication channels. The chances are, it's more costly than the value that seventh person *might* add. Don't forget your ruthlessness.

THE RIGHT PEOPLE

Keeping the numbers low and having all of the right people in the room is a delicate balance. In his book *Rebel Ideas,* Matthew Syed reminds us why we need diversity among our attendees. He gives examples of life and death situations and examples of civil unrest that were a result of having a lack of diversity of thought and experience in the room. Inviting people who are likely to have different backgrounds, experiences and thoughts will create better meeting results.

We met with a prospective client recently who was keen to fix their meetings culture. On asking more, it appeared that not only was the organisation having too many meetings, but in some cases the key people weren't attending. We asked why not and were given a list of really good possible reasons for their lack of attendance. We then asked if those people had actually been asked why they weren't there. They hadn't. We can assume and suppose, but if key people aren't coming to a meeting and you need them there, it's time for an honest conversation where you do most of the listening. Questions such as 'What do I need to do to get you to attend this meeting?' or 'We need your input on this, how would you like to give it?' could be good conversation starters.

TO CHAIR OR NOT TO CHAIR?

Very often, the reason why so many meetings can go horribly wrong or feel like a waste of time is that the selected chairperson isn't the most appropriate person for the role. Meetings are often chaired by the person who convened the meeting, rather than by someone who has the right skills. Have you been to meetings where the chairperson has a complete inability to keep the meeting on track? Or perhaps they have too much to say about the subjects under discussion?

If you are the person who has identified the need for a meeting, decide if you are the most appropriate person to chair the discussion. The first question to ask yourself is: 'Is my role to share information, or to engage in discussion?' If the answer is that you need to give information, for example make your colleagues aware of a problem and then involve them in solving it, being the chair could be a good role for you. If, on the other hand, you have a lot to say on the issue and want to be actively involved in problem-solving, then you might ask someone else to chair the discussion.

Handing over the car keys

Graham has been in situations where he invited external expert facilitators to help lead discussions or away days for his organisation. He starts off the day by introducing the facilitator, making it clear when they will be taking over. This is referred to as handing over the car keys. It's still Graham's car, but the facilitator's job is to temporarily drive for the day. This allows Graham to do two things: firstly, to participate; and secondly, to be aware of his team's response to the discussion or event. He can't possibly do all of this at once, as well as run the day, to the best of his ability. Involving someone else allows him to perform the roles needed for that meeting, while someone else facilitates it. At the end of the day, the facilitator hands back to Graham to wrap up – a metaphorical handing back of the car keys.

Pretty please ...

If you aren't going to be the chair, who can you ask? From time to time, it might be appropriate to invite someone external to facilitate the meeting. This is often the case when people are putting together new strategies, or learning new skills. As Productivity Ninjas we are often asked to facilitate in this way. If you are looking for someone internal, that might be someone on the team who is known to be a good listener and facilitator, or someone on another team whose knowledge commands respect. You could explain to them why you think having someone else chair the meeting would be a good idea, and perhaps even offer yourself or someone else to return the favour sometime.

EXERCISE: ROLE UP

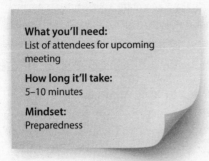

What you'll need:
List of attendees for upcoming meeting

How long it'll take:
5–10 minutes

Mindset:
Preparedness

Think about the particular skills people need to be good at performing each role.

Role	Qualities that would help this role
Chair	
Timekeeper	
Minute-taker	
Host	

If it's your meeting, you can allocate roles. Who do you have close by, in your team or in your networks, who you could lean on to help? (It also helps to think about playing to their natural strengths and enthusiasms, rather than just thinking 'who are my direct reports?'). Talk to people beforehand about what you would like them to do and why.

If it's not your meeting, do you want to offer to take on a role to help keep the meeting on track? This shows that you value the importance of the chair's role and want to help keep them focused. If you don't feel this is appropriate, perhaps observe the meeting and think about which roles could help next time and suggest this to the meeting leader.

MEETINGS MENU

Now that you have designed your meeting, with a purpose, a plan, protocols in place and the right people attending, you need to consider what the best format would be.

Below is our meetings format menu. You can mix them up depending on what works best – for some meetings you'll be looking for a starter, a main and perhaps even dessert. For other meetings one course will work well, and in other circumstances where there is more to cover, you might want to use different approaches for different areas of the agenda.

TRUTH AMNESTIES / BLOW SH*T UP

Purpose:

▶ Changing culture / habits

▶ Identifying barriers to success

▶ Improving working practices

The occasions where the whole team or business get together can be great opportunities to look at strategy and solve short-term challenges. But what about the stuff that never makes it onto the agenda? A truth amnesty can be a really powerful way of using some of your meeting time to scrutinise your culture and working environment. It was mentioned earlier as an approach used by BrewDog.

As we discussed earlier, at Think Productive we used part of our away day timetable for a truth amnesty. This was a point at which anyone could write down anything on a Post-it Note. There wasn't a theme, instead allowing people to express their thoughts on anything that we did, do, or have thought about doing as a company. It didn't need to be related to their role, or have anything to do with them personally. We didn't know who had written what, but each Post-it was then discussed, asking:

▶ Was it working?

▶ How could it work better?

▶ Should we scrap it?

It was great. We scrapped lots of things, ranging from annual leave entitlement for head office staff, to reviewing our presence on Twitter. We ditched a few meetings. We tasked a few people to look into some other stuff in more detail. It was very powerful. There was no blame, no one challenged the need for a discussion about any of the issues, and the pace was fast. Our HQ team does this regularly. It keeps the culture agile, allows people to ask 'why' and leads to finding a better way of doing things.

What would you mention if you were to have a truth amnesty? Try it out and see what happens. Think about who would need to be invited to make decisions or take actions.

DAILY HUDDLE

Purpose:
▶ For teams to update and support each other

▶ Reduces the need for more lengthy team meetings

The idea is that each day people get together for a short time, reducing the need for longer meetings. It gives colleagues an opportunity to check in with each other, see how people are doing and offer support as needed. This is ideal for fast-paced or responsive environments. Ideally it takes place at the same time, every day, standing up, and taking less than ten minutes. It's helpful to have a clear purpose statement and set of agenda questions, even if it happens every day. We've found that just adding the statement and questions to the appointment in everyone's shared calendars is the easiest way to do this (and it's great in case the regular chair is ill or away and you need someone to step up quickly).

CASE STUDY: THINK PRODUCTIVE

At Think Productive the UK HQ team has a daily huddle that covers these five questions:

1. How are you and what's your good news?

2. What are the figures? (We briefly summarise key sales data so that the team remain focused on this every day.)

3. What's your frog for today? (A frog is the thing you've been putting off doing. It comes from Mark Twain's quote: 'If it's your job to eat a frog, it's best to do it first thing in the morning. And if it's your job to eat two frogs, it's best to eat the biggest one first.')

4. Any stucks? (By this we mean, where do you feel like things aren't moving forwards and do you need help to get unstuck?)

5. Are we all OK for tomorrow?

Some team members are present to do the huddle in person, and others dial into the discussion. This happens at 9.30am, and to avoid any unnecessary interruptions, we ask Ninjas (that's what we call our trainers at Think Productive) to only call HQ between 9.30–9.40 if it really can't wait.

There is an optional 'Team Stuck hivemind' discussion for five minutes afterwards, which involves people whose 'stuck' might need some more thought and those who can help. Those who aren't involved are then able to crack on with their own work, and those who can assist are able to do just that.

We're increasingly being told that clients who huddle and focus on the targets and longer term objectives in this way find it really beneficial. One client now has a huddle three times a week: Monday to share priorities, Wednesday as an update on progress towards those priorities, and Friday to celebrate this work being done. How would you and your colleagues focus your attention differently if you were sharing what you were working on and your progress in this way?

Encourage people you work with to try out a daily huddle. If they are resistant, try it just for the next month and see if people want to keep it. Could this replace some of your other regular meetings?

Online or in person can work equally well for your huddle. Don't let the fact that your team is dispersed stop you.

SILENT MEETING

Purpose:

▶ Allow everyone to express their views, not dominated by individuals

▶ People can complete their thoughts and have some quality thinking time before the discussion begins

A silent meeting is where people use a shared document, such as in Google Docs or similar, to ask and answer questions and share their views and opinions. Alyssa Henry from Square (a financial services company) is an advocate for these meetings, stating: 'Lots of research says that minorities, women, remote employees, and introverts are talked over in meetings and/or have trouble getting their voice heard in traditional meeting culture. It sucks not only for the people that are disempowered by the traditional approach, but it sucks for those that unintentionally talk over/shut down conversation, and sucks for leaders that want to hear the best ideas but can't because folks are being shut down–usually unintentionally.'[11]

The format sounds weird, but we can see how this makes a difference. It's not about who is the loudest or most assertive. It's about people having the thinking space to articulate their ideas without being interrupted, and being able to read and share the ideas of others without needing to respond immediately.

An early focus group for this book was led as a silent meeting. We met online at the agreed time, introduced ourselves out loud and recapped the meeting's purpose (which had been sent to everyone previously). We then invited participants to log in to an online document that we had prepared in advance with a number of questions. Everyone typed up their thoughts and reflections, and in real time we were able to comment on their contributions and ask further questions. When this was done, we could easily see the points that everyone was in agreement with, and could pull out the points that needed further clarification.

We did talk, but not until everyone had shared their thoughts. It helped to focus the discussion and ensure an equal contribution. There were people taking part in the meeting who defined themselves as introverts and others who were much more extrovert. The interesting thing was that everyone liked the format. This was an online meeting, but it could equally be done in person. If you prefer pen and paper, you could do this with Post-it Notes or ask people to write comments on flip charts or white boards.

Duplication can be avoided as you see what others have said and don't need to add anything where you are in agreement. Those in the meeting can share their thoughts just as easily as those who are remote, or who can't make the meeting. Some may just want to share an idea without being involved in the wider decision making, or if someone is only interested in one aspect of the discussion, then that is all they need to contribute to. They don't need to read the rest of the document if they don't want to.

You could experiment with people adding their comments during the meeting, or have a go at people adding them before the meeting begins if this fits their schedule better. It's then possible for the meeting leader to pull out what needs further discussion.

BOARD MEETING

Purpose:
▶ To provide strategy, direction, compliance with legal framework, overseeing the financials and so on

▶ Often organisations will be required to have them

Board meetings are often non-negotiable, both in terms of frequency and numbers of people attending.

Very often they will be about approving things, making decisions on strategy and perhaps troubleshooting too.

The role of a board member, as with any meeting participant, is to challenge the status quo and ask if there is a better way. They need to question what they are hearing, check on assumptions being made and hold the executive to account for their work. They focus more on the strategic direction than the operational details.

Preparedness is key. Often board members won't be involved in the day-to-day running of a company and it takes time for them to understand how things work. A good induction for people on your board is crucial. We have both sat on a number of boards, some which performed this role well, challenging and taking on the role of critical friend. We have both left boards that simply provided a rubber stamp, or got into the nitty-gritty which isn't the role of a board at all.

Before people join a board, invite them to join in with one of the meetings – don't ask them to be silent observers. Your board needs critical creative thinkers, so encourage them to ask questions and get involved. How else will you know if they are any good in a meeting environment?

TEAM MEETINGS

Purpose:

▶ Troubleshooting

▶ Fostering collaboration that helps to achieve your goals

▶ Maintaining a well-informed and engaged team

Team meetings are an opportunity for members to share what is happening within their area of work. It's a place to solve problems and to be reminded that you are all working towards the same goal. It's a chance to anticipate what challenges lie around the corner and to be proactive about how to deal with them. Team meetings should be held frequently, perhaps monthly. They help to keep the work of the team as a whole on track, and to provide a sense of engagement, especially for remote workers.

Don't be tempted to use the same purpose statement for each meeting, or you may end up having the same conversation each time and it will quickly begin to feel stale. Make sure that you review and update the statement given the context of your meeting, and if you feel a meeting is not needed – skip it!

INTERNAL SUPERVISION / 1–2–1 MEETING

Purpose:
▶ Building key relationships

▶ Analysing and steering performance (more strategically than on a day-to-day basis)

We often hear people suggest that good meetings practice does not apply here. Argh! If you don't consider a meeting between yourself and your line manager to be worthy of your investment and attention, we don't know what is. If you are the line manager, this is an opportunity to help your staff member grow, develop, and to ensure they are doing their very best work and hold them to account.

The problem with these meetings is that they can often overrun, they lack focus and decisions are easily deferred because there are only two people involved.

TOP TIPS FOR 1-2-1 MEETINGS
▶ Share in advance the issues you would like to discuss – a purpose statement for two. If you forget or can't get someone else on board with that, make the list at the start of your meeting (like in the ad hoc catch-up meeting below).

▶ Hold your meeting in different locations. That can still apply if your meeting is online – you don't always need to be in the same place when you take the call.

▶ Have an agenda. Mix up the format of it from time to time.

▶ Stick to it. This isn't one to be moved about, cancelled and rescheduled. Value each other.

CATCH-UP MEETING

Purpose:
▶ Small, collaborative meetings between two or three people

For brief ad hoc meetings, or conversations where you want to keep it informal, the discussion should still have a purpose – otherwise you'd not be getting together, would you?

Both in person and online, these meetings can be difficult to keep short. Often beginning with an informal chat, it's easy for them to get stuck in that mode. The next thing you know, twenty minutes have passed and you've forgotten to talk about your reason for meeting. Whoops.

The beauty of these meetings, however, is that they often feel more collaborative. They may not have a clear chairperson, so appointing one can help keep you on track. We'd suggest that you remind yourselves early on why you wanted to get together in the first place. Make a list of what you want to achieve in your time together. Then decide if it's realistic. If it is, then crack on through your just-thought-out agenda. Just don't let this approach become the norm for how you meet. It generally means people are less prepared, making the meetings longer and less effective.

Limit the time – fifteen minutes for a brief catch up is usually adequate.

BRAINSTORMING MEETING

Purpose:

▶ An opportunity to come up with ideas, to be creative

These are a favourite of ours. You could record thoughts on a flip chart or divide people into groups to generate ideas.

You might want to ask participants to write their ideas on Post-it Notes to give everyone an equal say and avoid the discussion being dominated by just a few people. This is great for getting things moving quickly and it appeals to introverts. People who are more extroverted will generate ideas from talking with each other and building on one another's suggestions, and they will be able to do this once everyone has had a chance to write down their ideas.

One of the difficult things about brainstorming is that people often struggle to think beyond the everyday and their current working constraints. A tactic that can help is to ask people to imagine that they are setting up a new service, or offering a new product that competes with your own. There's rarely a struggle to think up ideas for improvement when there are no constraints around resources. You can then ask people to pick which of the ideas they would carry out if they had to deliver on a shoestring and ask them to justify why. Removing constraints and then putting them back is a sure-fire way to generate a wide variety of ideas.

These discussions are our kind of fun, but be sure to get clarity on who is responsible for taking things forwards and how.

EXERCISE: PICKING FROM THE MENU

What you'll need:
This chapter to refer back to, some way of making notes and your calendar

How long it'll take:
About 15 minutes

Mindset:
Unorthodoxy

Have a cup of tea or coffee with a colleague or business partner, and pick their brains about meeting formats. Ask them 'how can we make meetings more creative, interesting, productive and shorter?':

▶ Which of the meeting formats we've discussed feel the most interesting for you to try with your team?

▶ Are there any new ideas here that feel particularly daring or risky? If so, what would encourage you to be brave and give one of them a go?

▶ What's NOT working well at the moment for you and your team, and how might some of these formats shake things up and give your meetings a new flavour?

BUT I'M NOT THE ORGANISER! WHAT CAN I DO?

We've primarily focused so far on what you can do when you're the meeting organiser. However, that's not to say that you don't have a part to play even when it's someone else's meeting. In fact, being a role model as a meeting participant, and a constructive and thoughtful back-seat driver can be hugely influential. Here are a few thoughts on how to steer from the back seat and influence the meetings that you don't directly control.

'Lead from the back and let others believe that they are in front' – Nelson Mandela

I HAVE NO CONTROL ...

What if someone else is setting the agenda, and it's not working for you? Well, this is the time to exercise your ruthlessness. Let's think back to the yin and yang of meetings. We always need to balance the yin energy of deep listening with the yang energy of getting some actual work done.

If you feel that you have no choice other than to attend a meeting (often for political reasons), it helps to have some clarity about the meeting's agenda.

To improve your experience with these meetings, you can use phrases like:

- ▶ Your meeting conflicts with other priorities (or meetings), so it would help me to know more about what you need from me. That way I can reschedule my other commitments or find a way to get you the information that you need before the meeting.

- ▶ I'd love to come to your meeting on Friday. I've taken a look at the agenda. Can you tell me more about what you need in relation to X, Y and Z so I can best prepare? (Or find out if I am the right person to attend.)

▶ I know that you are really busy, so to make sure that I prepare well for your meeting and don't waste your time, can you tell me more about the purpose of the meeting / what the meeting is looking to achieve / exactly what would be useful to discuss in item 3 etc. (Delete as appropriate.)

We'd suggest a phone call or asking in person rather than by email to get a response. This allows you to ask questions, dig deeper and get more clarity. Be confident in asking these questions before you decide if you are attending or not. It will really help you to plan, prepare and deliver your best work.

IT'S GONNA BE A DULL ONE

There may be times when you are in an important meeting, and although there are good reasons for you being there, it's dull, or you are tired, or have something else on your mind. Or, it could be that there are strategic reasons for attending a meeting – perhaps it's an important client, or your boss has said that you have to be there – even if the content doesn't feel relevant to you.

You need to prepare for these meetings just like any other, if not more so. About twenty minutes before any meeting it's a good idea to sit down and do a brain dump. If you are already practicing some good Productivity Ninja habits you will be using a second brain tool to capture your actions. If you haven't discovered this yet, use a to-do list and note down all the stuff that's on your mind, in as much detail as possible – that client call that you were supposed to make, or the fact that it's your mother's birthday tomorrow and you still haven't posted her card. You don't need to organise these points right now if you don't have time, but you do need to be specific – this will help you to avoid being distracted by these thoughts during the meeting. For example, the client that you want to call should be noted down as *Call Sarah about presentation on Friday. What did she think of the slides?* rather than just making a note of the name *Sarah*.

By writing down your other commitments to come back to later, you will be better able to focus on the meeting itself.

ZOOM SHAKE SHAKE SHAKE THE ROOM!

There are a few ways you can prepare for online meetings that will help with your productivity in general. If it's a meeting that you don't think is valuable, and you really can't get out of it, then remember the yin and yang of meetings and opt for ruthless yang: it's possible for you to have your camera off and your mic muted – put your mind on more valuable things! Spend a few minutes in advance looking for paperwork, piling up emails that need responses in your inbox (or 'action folder' if you're a Productivity Ninja!) and that way you can get through the meeting doing something productive. We recommend keeping the tasks fairly light, so that you can still have half of your attention on the boring proceedings (mainly in case your name is called!). We want to emphasise that this is the last resort, for meetings that you absolutely have to be a part of but that you have identified as really not a good use of your energy. If you have a leadership role we would caution against this as it sets the wrong tone – use your leadership qualities to not be at the meeting in the first place or to question why it needs to happen.

If you are leading meetings and find that participants are doing this, then recognise that your meetings aren't working for them. Instigate conversations outside of the meeting and reevaluate if the people in question are needed next time. This could be a sign that things need shaking up in your meetings to re-engage people.

Let's turn now to the meetings you *do* want to be a part of. Take a few moments to make sure your space is quiet, brightly lit and that you've closed all other windows on your computer. For the same reasons we discussed earlier, we'd recommend putting your phone somewhere else to avoid distractions.

If you're not in control of the meeting's direction, but have certain key points that you want to get across, you can remind yourself of these with Post-it Notes on the wall behind your screen or on the edge of the screen itself. This means that you can maintain eye contact while making these points and appear more confident. Make the circumstances work for you.

DON'T THINK TWICE

Checklists can save you from making mistakes and can help you do things faster and with less stress. Unsurprisingly, we are fans. Hayley once worked with an event organiser who had a checklist for everything. This meant she only needed to think of something once – the next time she was in the same situation, she could just refer to the checklist because she'd done it all before.

BEFORE MEETING CHECKLIST

As a participant in a meeting, we suggest something along these lines for a 'before the meeting' checklist:

▶ Do I still want to attend? Does this meeting help me achieve my priorities?

▶ If I am still going, what do I want to get from it?

▶ What do I want to contribute?

▶ Has the purpose been set, and if not, what can I do to influence that?

▶ Have I read the agenda and any papers? If not, when will I do that? Could I do it now?

▶ What further information do I need to bring to the discussion?

▶ Is there likely to be tension around some of the issues? What can I do to contribute to those items in a positive way?

▶ Do I know how to use the online tools? Is everything installed on my machine?

▶ Will I have a quiet space to take part in the meeting online?

IF YOU ARE RUNNING THE MEETING:

▶ Do I have a defined and communicated purpose?

▶ Who do I really need there? How do I persuade them to attend?

▶ Is there an agenda with timings and is it clear what the purpose is for each point?

▶ Do people know what to prepare in advance (if anything)?

▶ Do we need refreshments?

▶ Do I have the right space booked?

▶ What can I do to show people their involvement is appreciated?

▶ Who is best placed to chair the meeting?

▶ What other roles will be needed?

▶ What are the sticking points likely to be? Who are my key influencers or 'allies' to help move the conversation on, or help establish consensus?

▶ Do we need paper copies of the agenda or not?

▶ Have people confirmed their attendance? Who do I need to chase up?

▶ How many people do I expect to attend? Does the plan (and room!) work for those numbers?

LOGISTICS CHECKLIST

▶ Do we have the right kit in place (projectors, flip charts etc.)?

► What's the room layout going to be (and do we have the right tables, chairs – and time! – to create the right layout)?

► Have we got access to water, glasses etc.?

► Are the refreshments arranged? Any specific requirements or allergies?

► For timekeeping, if there's a clock in the room, is it correct? Is the timekeeper working from that one, or from their own watch which is ten minutes faster? (There's a reason army generals in films start operations with 'Right. Synchronise watches!')

► If there are breaks, do any hosts or caterers know what the timings are for these? What's the wiggle room if things are running over, or if we want coffee ten minutes earlier?

FOR ONLINE MEETINGS:

► Does everyone know how to use the technology?

► Has everyone got the login details and any special instructions they might need?

► Is there a 'tech point of contact' (via phone/text/WhatsApp) so that if people can't log on, then assistance can be provided?

► What's the protocol if someone is having issues with their technology during the meeting? (e.g. 'Let us know via the chat if you can't hear us', or 'Text Elise if you have any tech issues.')

► For client meetings, board meetings and meetings that involve external participants, is there someone available (ideally who isn't in the meeting) who can be contacted by phone if there are major technical difficulties and someone can't join the meeting?

► If my own tech has a failure while I'm chairing, whose job is it to step in? Do I have a backup laptop/Zoom account/phone hotspot/etc. to get me back in quickly?

EXERCISE: MAKING A LIST, CHECKING IT TWICE

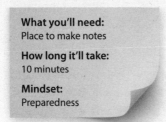

What you'll need:
Place to make notes

How long it'll take:
10 minutes

Mindset:
Preparedness

Draft your own pre-meetings checklist that reflects the kind of meetings that you attend and your responsibilities.

1.

2.

3.

4.

5.

YOU WILL KNOW THAT YOU ARE FIXING MEETINGS WHEN:

▶ You prepare well for meetings and know what you want to achieve from them.

▶ You ask questions of yourself and others before the meeting to help it run smoothly.

▶ You get the right people in the meeting, and don't attend if you aren't one of those people.

4.
DURING THE MEETING

If all is going according to plan, this is the moment when you meet with others and do some great work together. It could be a board meeting, a sales meeting, or a more informal team meeting. Perhaps it's online, or perhaps it's in person. Whatever shape and size it is, the actual meeting is most likely to be the part that people remember – hopefully for the right reasons.

SPRINT

If you have prepared and planned in advance, then the meeting itself should really be the easy bit. Think about Usain Bolt, the world record holder for the 100 metres. He doesn't just turn up on the day and deliver his best performance in 9.58 seconds by fluke. He has spent many, many years in intensive training, working with coaches, thinking about what he eats, and looking after his body and mind to become the fastest man on the planet. We're pretty sure he does some other complex stuff too, but as neither of us are champion sprinters we couldn't tell you what that is.

By the time Bolt turns up on the day of the race, he has already done all of the hard work. If he hasn't prepared, he can't just wing it on the day (and if he did, he wouldn't be the world champion). It's all the stuff you do before that takes the effort. The same is true of your meetings. This is why preparedness is so important.

The aim is to make your contribution count, helping to creating a decisive meeting that is focused on actions, collaboration and fulfilling the purpose that you have set.

If you are the meeting organiser, remember that other people have given up their energy, attention and time to be with you. This costs them, in terms of what they could be doing instead, so you owe it to them to make it count. It also costs the business money, so you need to be able to justify your outcomes to the budget holders. It's time to use your team's resources to the best possible effect.

The cost of a meeting is hard to measure, but apps such as Meeting Cost Timer for Android and Meeting Calculator for iPhone can be useful devices to try every once in a while. You simply download the app, enter the average salary for the people in the room, and watch the collective cost rack up as the meeting progresses, like a taxi meter stuck in a traffic jam.

WHAT YOU'LL FIND IN THIS CHAPTER

This chapter is broken into two sections. The first is aimed at meeting organisers or chairpeople. It includes some ideas and tips for how you can run the meeting, but there's still lots here to learn even if you're a meeting participant, including some ideas that the chair would appreciate your help with. The second section goes into more detail about how you can best engage in meetings as a participant, to deliver great work and get the most from other people.

FOR MEETING LEADERS

CHAIRING MEETINGS

The way we see it, the chair's role is to maintain the balance of yin and yang in a meeting. They need to make sure that the meeting's purpose is achieved by keeping everyone on track, enabling everyone to have their say while making sure that the conversation isn't dominated inappropriately.

For many people, especially those in more senior roles, several hours each week can be spent chairing meetings – yet in a job interview it's rarely asked about. Being a great chair is a transferrable skill that is often overlooked. It requires outstanding communication, deep empathy and excellent timekeeping. Most importantly, these skills can be learned, improved upon and used to make your working life easier, improve your reputation and your effectiveness.

Someone who's not very good at chairing is pretty easy to spot. A good chair, however, can deftly deal with a range of different behaviours, keep everyone focused and make it all look easy at the same time. Doing this for an online meeting is just as important, and perhaps requires even more effort.

THAT DRAGGED ON

We bet you've been to some meetings that lacked purpose, where you felt like you were wasting your time. Perhaps the conversation was going around in circles and you were hoping that someone else would wrap it up soon. If the meeting was online, you may have been fiddling with your phone or another web page. When leaving these meetings, you probably couldn't tell someone what you had been doing for the last two hours. You feel drained, unproductive and begin contemplating rewriting your CV. Chances are, these meetings were chaired by someone who was trying to take notes, be the timekeeper, and participate in discussion all at the same time, or by someone with poor chairing skills.

EXERCISE: WHAT MAKES A GOOD CHAIR

What you'll need:
Some way of taking notes

How long it'll take:
15 minutes

Mindset:
Preparedness

We want to turn you into an excellent chair. So, what does this involve? Think about a meeting you have been to where the chair did a great job. What did they do? How did it feel to take part? Make a list below:

1.

2.

3.

4.

5.

Looking over your list above, which of these things could you do more of in meetings, even when you aren't the chair? As an active participant, you don't have to wait for the chair to take the lead – you can ask questions, or move people on, or whatever else you need to do.

A brilliant chair will be doing many of these things:

▶ Starting the meeting on time

▶ Keeping everyone on track and aligned with the purpose of the meeting

▶ Making sure that the conversation isn't dominated by any individuals

▶ Moving the discussion on to avoid it getting repetitive, off-topic or just plain dull

▶ Sticking to the agenda unless there is a good reason not to

▶ Recognising what is and what isn't a good reason to move away from the agenda

▶ Being clear about what is expected from participants before, during and after the meeting

▶ Ensuring that everyone who wants to contribute has the opportunity to do so

▶ Making sure that actions are captured

▶ Recognising when energy or attention is reduced and taking action to address that

▶ Finishing the meeting on time (or ideally, early)

CHAIR? WHAT, ME?

You find yourself chairing a meeting. It could be that you got here by a well-planned strategy, or it may be that you have been thrown in at the deep end. Regardless of how you got here, you need to make this meeting work.

It's nice when the chair checks in at the start to ask if there is still a need for this meeting. Is the purpose still relevant? For example, there would be no point in the HR team meeting to discuss new recruitment methods if the CEO had announced that morning that 50% of staff are to be made redundant. It's good to confirm, during those first few moments, that there is still a need for the meeting and that people are still committed to the purpose.

LIGHTS, CAMERA, ACTION

When a meeting is online, as well as checking in at the start, the chair should also be making sure that everyone can see and hear each other. Using cameras as well as microphones is known to increase engagement – people are less tempted to do something else or allow their attention to wonder, and research shows that face-to-face meetings generate more ideas.[1]

STARTING WITH THE 4 PS

When you start your meeting, remind people what the 4 Ps are and how they will work in your meeting. A sentence around each will suffice.

4

⯅ PURPOSE
☰ PLAN
🚫 PROTOCOL
👥 PEOPLE

Purpose: Remind people of the meeting's purpose statement. If possible, have it on display so that attendees can refer back to it throughout the meeting.

Plan: Let people know how the meeting is laid out and the timing of any breaks.

Protocols: If you're online, do people know how best to conduct themselves? If meeting face to face, have you discussed the use of technology in the meeting?

People: It's really important to introduce people properly. Knowing who is who, and their role in the meeting is useful for everyone, even when people know one another.

Purpose, the place to start

Imagine if your monthly team meeting began with: *'We are meeting because we do this every month, someone once thought it was a good idea and none of us mentioned that it's not working for us any more.'*

How does that compare to: *'The purpose of this month's meeting is to find ways we can help each other to achieve this quarter's targets, as well as to plan for the new product launch in September.'* It's useful to remind people of the purpose of the meeting, even when they have the agenda in front of them. For meetings that happen regularly, the purpose should be for *this* meeting specifically.

Introductions. Who is that man with the moustache?

Do you remember your first few meetings in a new role? Chances are there were lots of acronyms to get used to and lots of new faces. Recalling not only names and faces, but who does what and how senior they are can be a real minefield for many. If there is a group of people who you only meet with monthly or quarterly, then this information is even harder to retain. That's why introductions are really important.

If you are at a meeting and the person chairing the discussion hasn't introduced everyone, you could suggest that it happens. People might not thank you out loud, but most will appreciate it.

Why am I here?

Ever ask yourself that in a meeting? Introductions can be a good way for people to be clear about why they are there in the first place, or understand why someone else is attending. Even if people know each other, it could be a good idea to ask people to introduce themselves and explain in a sentence why they are at the meeting and what they want to gain from it. For example, rather than Sally (Finance Manager) stating her name and job title, she might say: *'I'm Sally and I have overall responsibility for the finances. My role at the meeting today is to assist in planning the strategy for the next six months in a way that keeps us within the budget and makes best use of the resources we have.'* The advantage is twofold; everyone knows what Sally's role is, including Sally herself, who is stating her responsibilities in relation to the discussion.

Asking your timekeeper to give people a minute each (or less) will help keep this brief. Including this in the agenda, or giving people some warning that you will be doing this, is likely to increase the quality of the responses that you receive because people will have time to prepare.

Positively

Meetings often start with people listing all the things that they planned to do from the last meeting. Sometimes they've done them, sometimes they haven't, but it's not a particularly exciting start, is it?

Remember our concept of the 'opening round' when we talked about yin energy and deep listening in meetings? Asking everyone to speak about something positive early on helps to set expectations in two ways. Firstly, everyone knows they will be involved in the meeting, and secondly, sharing something positive has an impact on how they feel. The positive doesn't have to be related to the topic of the meeting, it can just help set the tone of the discussion. Limiting the time to 30 or 60 seconds can help create momentum. Ideas for your positive start could include asking:

▶ What is going well for you at work or in your life outside of work?

▶ What's gone well since our last meeting?

▶ What are you looking forward to about today (or this meeting, or this month)?

▶ What aspect of your work are you most excited about this week?

▶ What does success look like for you this week?

▶ For online meetings, you might want to ask people to share something about the space they are in; something they enjoy about it, for example.

TIME IS TICKING …

The chair doesn't have to be the timekeeper, but it's helpful if they can see a clock from where they are sitting. Sometimes looking at your watch while chairing the meeting can signify that time is short, which can help keep everyone on track, but constantly looking at your watch can be interpreted as lack of engagement, which isn't a good way to run a meeting. Let the timekeeper be responsible for giving reminders when time is short, or for timing each agenda point.

Timing the meeting or agenda

Think about the last time that you were in a meeting that overran. Can you remember how you felt? Most of the time, people are itching to leave, thinking about what else they were supposed to be doing by that point. Being aware, as the chair, that people have agreed to give their attention for a set period of time gives you an incentive for keeping the discussion to time. You have other stuff to do as well, right?

A good chair will recognise when the conversation needs limiting. To do that, you need to know the purpose behind the meeting and how the items on the agenda are going to get you to that conclusion. Breaking down each agenda item to show how much time to spend on it will provide momentum, reminding everyone that time is limited.

If the meeting is online, sharing the agenda and the purpose of the meeting at the start, on screen (and updating if needed), is a great visual cue and reminder that you are all starting from the same point.

CLOSURE

Ideally you will be looking to wrap things up about ten minutes before you want the meeting to end. You could say something along the lines of: *'OK everyone, we've had a great discussion, but we now need to make a decision. I see our options as being A, B and C. Have I missed anything?'* You might ask for a show of hands for each option. This technique could result in your meeting finishing even earlier.

Other things that you might say to help with closure:

▶ *'Good discussion everyone, thanks for your ideas. Now we need to clarify the action we are going to take.'* Then go around the room and ask people to share their actions. Others, including the person you have identified to take notes, can be encouraged to add things that people have missed. Always warn your note-taker at the start that you might do this, so that they can prepare.

▶ *'Let's clarify what actions we have come up with'.* Ask the note-taker to do this, or look at your shared list of actions if you've been using a silent meeting.

▶ *'I'm aware of the time, what else do we need to do?'*

Once the formal business has been done, it's always nice to end on a high. Ask people to share something positive that has come from the meeting, or something that they are looking forward to doing.

At a recent public workshop, we had a lot more participants than usual and wanted to keep the closing round short. A colleague suggested that we do a one-word closing round, asking people to state how they were feeling at the end of the course. People used words like motivated, focused, clear, inspired, positive, happy. What a positive way to end the day, that takes up very little time. You could also ask questions like:

▶ What did you learn?

▶ What did you value?

▶ What are you looking forward to?

▶ What have you appreciated about this meeting?

Or get people to complete a sentence, such as:

▶ That was a great meeting. It would be even better if ...

Remember that these things can either be verbalised, or written down in a shared space, for both in-person and online meetings.

POWER OF THE PAUSE

There is power in a pause. Think about watching a psychological thriller movie – it's the pause, the moment just before someone opens the door, when the tension peaks. Or if you're a music fan, sometimes hearing a pause where you should hear a note or a beat can be a thrilling way to make silence seem like the most musical thing in the world. In both of these examples, pauses are not pointless voids of nothing, but are filled with meaning. In meetings, pauses of silence can be a great way to allow ideas to settle.

When you see a masterful chair or facilitator at work, one of the things you'll often notice is how well they use the power of the pause. Pauses are helpful in three main ways:

1. Practical Pauses – whether scheduled or unscheduled, a pause can help people to replenish their energy levels when it feels like things are flagging.

2. Strategic Pauses – a pause can be a great way to diffuse tension if there is disagreement, or if the conversation is going around in circles.

3. Reflective Pauses – when there's a lot to take in, it can be helpful to allow everyone the space to digest, take notes, or just let their minds rest.

Let's look at a few pause tactics in detail:

1. PRACTICAL PAUSES: CAN I GO FOR A WEE, PLEASE?

Steve Jobs famously ran his Apple keynote talks using the 'ten minute rule': introduce something new every ten minutes, whether that's a new speaker, a piece of video, or some other break to the monologue. Why? Because he knew that people's attention spans were short. In an ideal world, all meetings would be so short that a break isn't needed, but even when using the ten minute rule, it's worth having a proper break an hour or so into meeting proceedings (and every hour after that if it's an all-day meeting).

You can often tell when people are ready for a break – they fidget, become less animated, and the energy dips. This is much harder to gauge in virtual meetings, so perhaps set yourself some reminders to check in with people periodically. If you have a longer meeting, it's a good idea to let people know when the break will be at the start.

We've heard a colleague say, 'No one's work idea is more interesting than a full bladder.' Sometimes you might just need to add in unscheduled breaks so people can go to the toilet, or get more water (or both). Hayley has been to events where, in addition to a scheduled break, the host has suggested a 'five minute leg stretch.' Yep, it takes longer than five minutes if it's a big group of people, but it really helps give people a quick comfort break. In our experience, if you see one or two members of a large group getting up to go to the toilet, it's worth declaring a break for everyone straight away. Seek consensus, and don't be afraid to ask if it might be a good time for an extra break (but remember they *want* you to take the lead, too).

2. STRATEGIC PAUSES

Practical breaks are important, but breaks can be about more than just biology. They allow people to reflect, especially if the conversation has become heated or a particularly thorny issue has been raised. In debates or disagreements, what tends to happen is that both sides will 'entrench' and 'escalate'. In other words, the longer a disagreement festers, the more likely you are to lose control of it. By having a break during a debate or disagreement, you allow everyone a chance to step away and pause. What we often find here is that the quieter, more reasonable or more pragmatic members of a group will use this moment to help mediate. At the same time, those at the heart of the debate will cool off a little bit, and they have a few precious moments to work out the kind of solution they would be happy with.

Strategic pauses are also wonderful for finding clarity. They allow us to find new ideas, to better evaluate information, and can even change our decision making. Research shows that taking breaks can affect the decisions that judges make about releasing prisoners: the sooner after a break the ruling is, the more likely the prisoner is to receive parole.[2] We all need to stop and recharge sometimes in order to make good decisions.

You don't need to order an extra coffee or toilet break to bring about a strategic pause. Instead, you can:

▶ Break out into small groups to look at different angles, or focus on different areas of the problem (stakeholders, budgets, options, pros and cons etc.).

▶ Go around the table and ask each person to summarise their thoughts and feelings so far (in one sentence, or one word if that feels appropriate). For example, are they currently thinking that they would vote yes, or no to a certain decision? Are they confident or concerned? You might remind people of the purpose, and ask where they think the meeting is at with achieving it.

▶ Ask everyone to write their ideas or solutions down on paper (or on their phone/laptop) in silence.

▶ Lead a very short meditation.

▶ Continue the discussion, but as the chair, consciously take the spotlight back for a few moments. Summarise things with a much quieter voice and slower pace than you've been hearing in the room (it helps, particularly if things have become heated, to exaggerate this – it's likely that there's enough adrenaline flowing that you'll already be talking slightly faster than normal). This jolting change of dynamic in the room will often act as a kind of pause, even without the need for you to take an actual break or disrupt the overall flow.

3. REFLECTIVE PAUSES

There is power in just asking everyone to pause from talking. This allows people a moment to reflect, taking into account the contributions that have been heard so far. Using a short meditation at the start or end of a meeting can be a good way to help people to be present in the discussion.

SHUT THE F**K UP

You may attend some meetings where you feel like you're constantly trying to find an opportunity to cut in, to say something and contribute. When people are always interrupting each other, you only get to share half-thought-out ideas. Many of our ideas develop and improve as we say them out loud, and by interrupting each other we don't allow time for our own thoughts and the thoughts of others to do this. That's where a pause can come in handy.

Pauses can also help when people aren't contributing. You just need to hold your nerve to get comfortable with silence. Most people will want to fill the silence and start contributing. The police use this as an interview technique, and counsellors use this to give people time to order and articulate their thoughts.

ENERGISING THE ATTENTION

There are many ways to press 'restart' on people's attention. Hayley had a lecturer at university who stopped talking every 25 minutes, so that students could talk among themselves for five minutes. This method, known as the Pomodoro Technique, lets people switch off briefly, and then come back to the lecture ready to focus again. Could you try this in a meeting?

Likewise, just shifting focus from a conversation to a quick video clip or 'show and tell' can be a really good way to break things up. Graham used to sit on the board of a national charity, where every board meeting would include a presentation from a member of the staff or a beneficiary who wasn't part of the board. These short items were usually a way to bring the board's thoughts back to the purpose of the charity (it can be easy to lose sight of the difference you're trying to make when you're deep into analysing the annual accounts or discussing a legal dispute!).

BRINGING THE FUN

There are loads of things that organisers can do to make meetings more effective, but there are also ways to lighten them up and make them more fun. And guess what? This helps people to focus better, engage in the discussion and remember the meeting.

MANAGERS CAN HAVE FUN TOO!

Some people think that having senior people in the meeting means that it should be less 'fun'. But why? The more senior someone is, the more likely it is that they have to spend large amounts of time in meetings and would appreciate a little fun thrown in. Obviously this is not suitable for all meetings (such as telling someone that they are going to be losing their job, disciplinary meetings and the like), but we challenge you to give some of these ideas a try in your team meetings, away days and any other meeting that could benefit from an injection of fun. Some have been tested out by clients, some we've read about along the way, and others just sound like a great idea and we'd love you to try them out:

▶ Start with something silly, perhaps a brief YouTube clip that makes people smile. It lightens the mood and only takes a couple of minutes. We know of a company that delegates this task to people who are late for a regular meeting – they have to pick the clip for the next time.

▶ Doodling. Why not award a prize at the end of the meeting for the best doodle? Having something to do while listening helps concentration and focus. This isn't the same as multitasking during meetings, which is not at all helpful.

▶ If you have someone taking notes, have a go at doing this using pictures. There are people who you can invite to your meeting to do this professionally – it's ideal for away days and bigger events (https://www.scriberia.co.uk).

▶ A quick game of musical chairs, twenty minutes in to the meeting, to get people moving and to potentially shake up some new ideas.

▶ Rhyme time. Have an item on the agenda where people need to make their points rhyme.

▶ Give out prizes during the meeting. You could have a prize for the best dressed attendee, the person with the most unorthodox idea, or the person who can use a pre-agreed word the most during a meeting.

▶ Have words in a meeting that are banned. People have to find an alternative, and there could be some sort of forfeit for slipping up. This could be a way to avoid jargon and TLAs (three letter acronyms), and is especially useful if new people are joining the discussion.

▶ Playing catch. If someone wants to speak, they can only do so when they have the ball (Microsoft use a rubber chicken nicknamed Ralph). This means that you can't interrupt or talk over people.

▶ We all know that snacks go down well in meetings. Give meeting participants an After Eight mint (ideally from the fridge). They place it on their forehead, and have to get it into their mouths without touching it, using only their face muscles. It will certainly lighten the mood and provide a hilarious few minutes of entertainment!

Some of these suggestions are pretty silly, but others work really well. How much fun and silliness can your meeting handle? Which meetings could benefit from more fun? Feel free to blame us for testing these things out.

DOMINATING THE DANCE FLOOR

When we deliver workshops we often find that one person contributes more than others. Sometimes that's OK as it gets the conversation going, but other times it's at the expense of others getting their say, which can cause frustration and zoning out. Often the person who is dominating isn't aware that they are doing it, or they are especially passionate about what's being discussed. Perhaps they just don't like the silence that results when a group is asked a question, and they want to fill that space before others have had a chance to think about what their answer might be. There are tactics that you can use, either as a meeting organiser or participant, to reduce the level of disruption that comes from one person dominating the proceedings.

IF YOU DON'T WANT TO DOMINATE

Perhaps you are a chatty extrovert, or you're in a meeting that is about your pet project. Either way, there will be times when you become aware that you are the person dominating the conversation.

If you start to notice that you are taking up more than your fair share of talking time, try some of the following:

▶ Note down your ideas as they come to you. Wait. Pausing allows others to speak up and share their ideas. By noting your ideas down, you can make your point succinctly when the time is right.

▶ Use phrases like 'I've already contributed a lot today, who else would like to?'

▶ Perhaps wait until last, sharing your point before moving on to the next agenda item.

IF YOU AREN'T CHAIRING AND SOMEONE ELSE IS DOMINATING

Perhaps the chair hasn't noticed, or they aren't doing anything about it, or perhaps they themselves are dominating the conversation. Most of the time, the chair will be grateful for the intervention of others to deal with this, and the other participants certainly will be.

You could try noticing when someone else looks like they want to contribute, and say something along the lines of: 'Before you go on, Paul, I think Martin had something to add or ask?'. Alternatively, you could summarise what has been said, and ask if anyone took any other points from Paul's contribution. While it might not feel like your place to do this if you aren't chairing, you still have an important role as a participant to speak up. If something's not working for you, it's likely to not be working for others too, and they will thank you (if only silently).

TACTICS FOR CHAIRING WHEN PEOPLE ARE TOO VOCAL, OR TOO QUIET:

▶ Use Post-it Notes. Hand them out to everyone and ask them to work individually to contribute their thoughts, ideas or questions. Group similar ideas and themes together for further discussion, and then allow people to add their comments and thoughts on each theme/idea to a flip chart. The chair can summarise these and identify the areas that still need further discussion. There are tools that will allow you to do this online too. You can use a shared document, or the chat area that most online meeting tools have, allowing everyone to see each other's contributions.

▶ Give people specific questions to discuss in pairs. Ask people to change pairs often so that individuals don't get stuck with someone who dominates or who they just don't work well with. This can work online too. Individuals can mute themselves (to save the hassle and time delays of logging on and off) and use phone calls or messaging tools to speak in smaller groups.

▶ Go around the room and ask everyone to share their comments on the item being discussed in turn. It's fine for people to pass if they have nothing new to add.

MOVE IT

Encourage movement. In our workshops we often ask people to move seats every so often, or to stand for discussions that last less than ten minutes. This gets blood moving around the body, which we know increases the energy of the group. You could try standing meetings, walking discussions, or agenda items where you move seats. In 1999, the Journal of Applied Psychology found that sit-down meetings lasted 35% longer than those held standing up, and there was no difference in effectiveness.[3] As standing desks are on the increase, we hope that standing meetings start to be too.

If you can't make your whole meeting a standing one, perhaps allocate some agenda items to be discussed standing up. Watch and feel how the energy in the room increases.

How can you get creative with movement in meetings?

CAR PARKS OR PARKING LOT

Sometimes a conversation isn't relevant to the agenda or meeting purpose, but is useful to the wider team or organisation.

This is where 'parking the idea' can be really useful. Let's give you an example. We were delivering a Getting Your Inbox to Zero workshop with a client who had booked a lunch for participants after the session to give feedback, and to discuss how email and instant messaging were used in their culture. During the workshop, several issues were raised about practices that varied, expectations that were different in separate parts of the business, or just wildly different expectations held by individuals. In order not to lose those issues, knowing that there was to be a further discussion around this at lunch, we captured them on a flip chart. The issues included things that were less about how individuals dealt with their own emails (which the workshop gave solutions for), but rather about the expectations held by others. For example, the fact that some people were looking at and responding to emails while on holiday, that people were sending each other WhatsApp messages at 11pm to get things off their mind, and that some people felt ten minutes was a reasonable time within which to respond to an email, whereas others felt three days was acceptable. There was a clear lack of clarity on how communication should work at the organisation. By capturing these issues on a flip chart, we kept the actual session on track, but also didn't forget to discuss the problems around expectations within the company's culture.

You can do this visually if you are meeting in person, or by creating a slide that others can see if you are in an online meeting. It might be a good idea to ask someone other than the minute-taker, chair, or timekeeper to be responsible for this.

For face-to-face meetings, having a white board or flip chart with 'car park' written at the top will start you off. If, for example, the purpose of your meeting is to decide how staff induction processes are to be improved, and it is highlighted that there is a delay with adding people to payroll, this is an important issue. However, it's not moving you towards your goal. By 'parking' the idea on the white board or flip chart during the meeting, you can then spend a few minutes at the end allocating tasks around these issues or deciding which need to make it to future meetings. Ask people to update on progress outside of the meeting if it's that important. Or even better, let people know that everyone should assume those items are dealt with unless the person reports back that they need help. If it can be dealt with outside of a meeting, then that should be the first choice.

MOVE ALONG NOW

Sometimes a meeting can get a bit stuck. Everyone, not just the chair, can get involved in helping to move the discussion onwards. Some ideas for phrases to use in these situations include:

▶ 'My understanding is that we have agreed X and Y. Which leaves us to figure out Z.'

▶ 'Now that we've had a discussion, it sounds like we could do one thing or the other. Should we take a vote?' (If it's not a meeting where voting feels right, suggest that people say which option they prefer, or clarify how the decision will be made and communicated to everyone.)

▶ 'We've been discussing this for a while now, and it sounds like everyone has had their say. Whose decision is it ultimately?'

▶ 'We've heard from most people, is there anything someone else would like to add?'

▶ 'We are running out of time here. We have two minutes to identify who will be taking this forward outside of the meeting.'

▶ 'I'm looking at the time, let's move on.'

▶ 'The actions we have so far on this are...' (Ask the note-taker to clarify the actions.)

▶ 'Let's go around the room. If you could only do one thing about this issue, what would you do and why?'

MANAGING THE HIPPO EFFECT

Avinash Kaushik was the first person to name the HiPPO (Highest Paid Person's Opinion) effect, to describe what happens when the person with the highest salary or the most experience voices their opinion. He notes that even if the data doesn't support this person's view, people are less likely to speak out against it and therefore often go along with it. This is something we notice a lot in our Think Productive workshops: HiPPOs have influence, and while that's often born out of their direct experiences, it can skew the conversation in unhelpful ways. It is important to be mindful of this because meetings are a collaborative effort, where each person's opinions and expertise should be valued in the decision-making process – that's why they were brought together for the meeting in the first place. After all, no matter how good they are, the HiPPO can't possibly know everything and be right all of the time. Perhaps it's best to leave the views of the HiPPO until last, so that others can share their ideas without being influenced.

ME, I'M THE HIPPO

But what if you are the HiPPO? It's quite possible to still be involved and have your say. You could wait until you have heard everyone else's thoughts and then speak up if you have something to add. In very hierarchal organisations, the HiPPO effect is more likely to be a challenge.

Here are a few ways that, as a HiPPO, you can lessen the effect:

▶ Consciously make the decision to speak last in the group

▶ Be humble in your contributions

▶ Ask more questions than you give answers

▶ Dish out lots of praise for other peoples' ideas

▶ Remember the old Harry Truman quote: 'It's amazing what you can accomplish if you do not care who gets the credit'

▶ Actively seek diversity of ideas and opinions – ask who disagrees and empower critical thinkers who might not be confident enough to speak up without the prompt.

The other alternative is to take more of a coaching style. It might take a bit longer, but could be a way for people to develop their analytical thinking. In this approach, the HiPPO doesn't voice their opinion, but asks questions instead to encourage people to think differently and more critically. Here's an example:

We worked with a client whose company was a fast-growing start-up business. The founder was the CEO, and was very passionate about everything to do with her business. She found herself attending a lot of internal meetings because that way she could be involved in the discussion and sign things off. She came to Think Productive for the same reason that most of our clients do – there aren't enough hours in the day, and there were too many meetings preventing her from getting actual work done – work that only she was able to do. We suggested that each meeting have a clear purpose and that she only needed to attend for the last ten minutes. The rest of the meeting would be for the people at the operational level to be involved in the debate and discussion, and they'd put their recommendations to her at the end. She could then ask questions, to which they hopefully had the answer and she could sign off on their decision. This meant that the meeting had a clear brief, the HiPPO effect was minimised, and it resulted in the CEO spending less time in meetings.

DECISIVE

At the end of the day, if the purpose of a meeting is to reach a conclusion, someone somewhere needs to make the decision: being clear on who that is at the start of the meeting can be helpful. If the approach becomes to just do what the HiPPO says, simply because they are the HiPPO, the collaborative process of meeting with each other to share ideas and critique options becomes a pointless waste of time.

EXERCISE: HiPPO-SPOTTING

What you'll need:
Diary to remind you of your meetings and something to take notes with

How long it'll take:
5 minutes

Mindset:
Mindfulness

▶ Do I attend any meetings where the HiPPO effect is alive and well?

▶ If the answer is yes, does something need to be done to change the dynamic of that meeting? What can I do?

▶ If I am the HiPPO, what can I do differently to show that I value and respect the contributions of others?

CONSTRAINTS

Putting constraints around meetings sounds like it will make them more difficult, but in fact it can be hugely helpful. It's often said that necessity is the mother of invention, and having less time, fewer people, a lower budget or other constraints can focus the mind on the best way to tackle an issue. The same is true for meetings. We'd like you to play around with your constraints a bit more in meetings. Time is an obvious constraint, so the first tip is to get strict on this. No more meetings that overrun – the meeting ends on time, or ideally sooner.

The number of people attending sounds like another obvious constraint, as does the frequency of meetings. But what would happen if you were to add in some more? No interrupting, for example? Or, perhaps allocating everyone a certain number of times they can speak (uninterrupted) during the meeting. This could be interesting, as could passing one of your turns to someone else if you would like to hear more about what they have to say.

Other ways to use constraints in order to have a more effective meeting include:

▶ Using the Pomodoro Technique, which involves taking a five-minute break every 25 minutes.

▶ Asking for responses to questions in one word or one sentence.

▶ Setting a timer for contributions, introductions or Any Other Business.

▶ Allowing people to speak for the length of time it takes the person on their right to walk around the room. You could have fun with this by slowing your pace if you want to hear more, or moving much faster if you've heard enough.

▶ Asking people to take it in turns to speak, but only for the length of time they can balance a book on their head (or stand on one leg, or something similar). Be sure to make this inclusive.

▶ Getting people to summarise their thoughts and ideas on one Post-it Note. Everyone can then view these and move them about to cast their votes.

MAKE BETTER DECISIONS

Edward de Bono's Six Thinking Hats is another tool you can use in meetings to improve your decision-making processes. Speedo are reported to have used the Six Thinking Hats technique to develop their swimwear for Olympic swimmers.[4] De Bono's model involves everyone wearing the same (imaginary) hat at the same time to explore different aspects of a problem:

▶ Blue hat (managing); defining the question and setting a goal. Taking a look at the problem in a wider context.

▶ White hat (information); looking at the data and exploring the facts.

▶ Red hat (emotions); how people feel about things without the need for justification or evidence. What are their gut reactions?

▶ Black hat (discernment); looking at what is practical and realistic. Identifying areas for caution.

▶ Yellow hat (optimistic); seeing the best possible solution, seeking harmony.

▶ Green hat (creative); being innovative, thinking about things in the most creative ways without any objections.

The Six Thinking Hats can be a great tool to use when emotions are running high. It allows discussion to follow a format that will address these emotions, giving them an opportunity to be considered alongside the facts, the creative solutions and the practicalities. By separating these different styles of thinking and taking them one at a time, everyone is made to consider and explore the same information together. This means that conflict is reduced and people have a lens through which to view a challenge or proposal. A decision can then be made, taking into account all of these different aspects which have been considered in detail.

MORE HATS

We love de Bono's Six Hats model, but you might want to consider other hats to wear. Organisations who are funded with public money will often ask 'does this pass the *Daily Mail* test?' (i.e. how would it appear sensationalised in the tabloids?) Other hats could include: what will the senior management team or board members want to know? How does this work from the customer's point of view? How does this work in terms of our own internal processes? What would our competitors do? What would a bigger (or smaller) business do? How do we approach this problem using our core values?

Think about the different hats that you could use to see a challenge from a different perspective.

DEALING WITH CONFLICT

Some people love a good debate that sparks conversation and perhaps even thrive on a bit of conflict. Most people shy away from it because it feels uncomfortable and difficult. The truth is that constructive disagreement and conflict can sometimes be necessary to reach a resolution. If the conflict isn't moving you towards your meeting's purpose, park it and come back to it outside of the meeting. If it is central to the discussion, you need to deal with it.

Ed Catmull (the founder of Pixar) is a great believer in inviting and encouraging feedback, which in many environments leads to conflict. He talks about the 'Braintrust' at Pixar, where a group of senior producers and experts will gather to watch an early draft of a film. They then go through it in detail, picking out all of the things that they believe are wrong with it. There is an opportunity here for conflict to arise, but it's encouraged – people are reminded that they are working together to make the film the very best it can be.

Often the best ideas will generate conflict, so we need to try and get comfortable with it. The silent meeting tool could help (p. 105), and other tips include:

▶ Pauses

▶ Pass the ball or chicken (p. 140)

▶ De Bono's Thinking Hats (p. 150)

▶ Reminding people to listen respectfully to each other

▶ Dividing into smaller groups

▶ Asking participants who disagree with each other to articulate each other's point of view, in order to build empathy

▶ Asking 'what do others think?' to the wider group

▶ Depersonalising where possible. Stick to the facts and talk about the different options, rather than asking who agrees with whom

▶ Having pre-meeting chats: as a chair, if you know there are a couple of people who will disagree on a certain issue, it's worth calling them up or visiting their desk and running through their concerns beforehand. This does two things: firstly, it gives them a chance to vent about the issue, which might help them feel less strongly at the meeting itself, or at least help them get their thoughts in order. Secondly, it also helps you as the chair to see both sides of the argument ahead of time, so that you can be prepared and form your own conclusions.

The above tips help to manage the healthy kind of conflict: professional disagreement over issues and ideas. People can disagree respectfully, with no personal offence taken, often leading to better conclusions.

However, within any work environment, other conflicts can arise: power struggles, clashing egos and genuine dislikes. People often feel uncomfortable when these conflicts are on display. Getting to know your colleagues, their styles of communication and how they work with each other will help anticipate these issues. Remember, you're there to contribute to the purpose of the meeting (whether you're the chair or a participant), so one of the best ways to diffuse these kinds of situations is to bring the attention back to the purpose statement and ask the question: 'Is this the best place to be having this discussion and does it help us meet the purpose of the meeting?'. If it doesn't, your best option is to try to move the conversation on (and let them simmer away with their conflict at some other time and place).

EXERCISE: CONFLICT: HEALTHY OR UNHEALTHY?

What you'll need:
Note-taking items

How long it'll take:
15 minutes

Mindset:
Preparedness

All participants in a meeting have a role to play in helping to keep conflict constructive. Conflict shouldn't always be shied away from as it can be healthy, but if dealt with badly it can be toxic for teams.

Think about the times you've experienced conflict in a meeting – whether you were involved in the conflict yourself, or witnessed it happening between others (where it wasted your time etc.).

Reflect on what could have been different in those situations. What was impressive in the way others dealt with it? What could you learn and do differently in the future?

10 WAYS TO MAKE MEETINGS A SUCCESS IF YOU'RE A PARTICIPANT

One of the key things that delegates take away from our workshops is that participants have a responsibility to make sure the meeting goes well: it's not just down to chair or organiser to ensure that people contribute and to help achieve the meeting's purpose.

Going to someone else's meeting isn't like going to the cinema, where we turn up to relax, switch off and expect to be entertained. Instead, think of accepting the invitation as joining a team of people working towards a common goal. Everyone has their part to play. That includes you – even if you have no specific role assigned. You need to manage your attention and energy levels so that you can engage and be a productive participant. Sometimes that's harder than it sounds.

The rest of this chapter will look at how meeting participants can think and act in a way that makes them an asset to every meeting. We'll look at what we physically do during a meeting and consider how we can think differently to be active and engaged in all meetings.

1. THINK ABOUT THE PHYSICAL (ENERGY BRINGS ATTENTION)

If you've decided to go to a meeting because it's important and helps you to achieve your goals, you want to be able to maintain your energy levels and focus during it. This isn't going to be the time for daydreaming about your next holiday.

Once you are in the meeting, think about how to best focus your attention. Hayley has some back pain and will often need to stand in a meeting. A side effect of this is that it helps her to stay focused

– sometimes changing the view can be useful. If your meeting is online, this can work really well. Stand for some agenda items and sit for others. If it's a longer meeting, and especially if you are working from home, try to move to different parts of your home or office for different bits of the meeting. This will help to keep you focused.

Graham's previous book, *How to Have the Energy*, is full of recommendations for how nutrition and hydration will help power your brain. Even a small amount of dehydration can play a big role in reducing your brain's performance. Getting caffeine and sugar intakes under control, so that your energy isn't spiked by peaks and troughs, will help too.

2. DOODLE

We love to doodle. Hayley's been to meetings and conferences where people will comment on her doodles. Once she was asked if she was an artist (they clearly couldn't see her doodles all that well), but most often, someone will ask if she is bored, or if the meeting was 'not her thing?'.

Mike Parker, CEO of Nike, is reported to be a doodler too, bringing a sketch book with him to meetings. He apparently uses the page on the left for brainstorming, while using the right-hand side for drawing and doodling.

In her TED Talk, Sunni Brown (author, entrepreneur and expert doodler), sheds some light on the matter. She explains how doodling is often seen as being 'anti-intellectual', but in fact there is research to back up that doodling helps you retain the information being discussed while you scribble. Doodling encourages you to engage – it is 'making spontaneous marks on paper that help you to think'.[5] In a study by psychologist Jackie Andrade, doodlers were able to retain 29% more information than non-doodlers.[6]

3. CHAIRS, THE KIND YOU SIT ON

Where people sit in a room can be important; we talked earlier about the difference between a formal boardroom and a circle of chairs, and the different dynamics these set-ups create. If you are joining an in-person meeting where you know that there is likely to be disagreement, you may prefer to sit with your allies, but the meeting would benefit from you mixing up the group so that you're not all unwittingly creating 'trench warfare' across the table. If there is someone you want to build relationships with, or make feel welcome, you might sit with them. If you're in one room all day, listening to various PowerPoint presentations or long contributions and there's a risk that they all start to merge into one, then moving chairs or changing your view will help to hold more of the discussion in your memory.

4. STANDING UP (OR STANDING MEETING)

We've all heard the notion that 'sitting is the new smoking'. If you're feeling tired or a bit brain-dead during a meeting, then stretching your legs by going to the toilet is a good way to get the blood flowing back to your brain without feeling out of place. If you're a little braver, you could suggest that you be allowed to stand for a while in the meeting, or even braver still, ask the entire group to stand!

5. TAKE YOUR OWN NOTES

Do you ever look back at the notes you took during a meeting? Many people don't refer back to them at all, and for those that do, it can just be jumble of words that don't make a lot of sense.

However, they can have their benefits. The main thing, of course, should be that they are useful for you. As a rough guide, you might want to think about:

▶ Noting information that is new to you, to decide what, if anything, you need to do with it later. The decision is an action for later.

▶ Jotting down things that you have been asked to take forwards. Be clear on what these things are, when they are expected and who needs to know about them.

▶ Things that aren't an action for you, but you might want to be informed of progress on. If you ask in the meeting to be kept updated, perhaps check that this is noted in the actions list at the end.

▶ Making a note of things that don't relate to the meeting, but that pop into your head. Then add these to your second brain later on. If you can note these things down before the meeting, it should help avoid them interrupting your thoughts.

▶ Creating a glossary of jargon and TLAs (Three Letter Acronyms). This is especially useful if you are meeting in a new environment or sector, as it will allow you to follow the discussion more easily. Add them in as you go along to create a quick reference tool.

Think about the meetings you have been to in the last two or three weeks. What were your actions? Were these clear? Did you note them down at the time? Relying on someone else to take notes of your actions can lead to misunderstanding, and usually the person who looks bad is you.

Another useful tip is to try to capture all of your actions in one place. If using paper notes, scan them in and store them electronically to make them easier to find at a later date.

6. THINK ABOUT YOUR PURPOSE (BEING MET)

By being clear on why *you* are attending a meeting, you can make sure that you achieve your purpose, even if others aren't sure what is going on. So even if the meeting doesn't have a purpose statement, and you've not sought one out, your planning should include creating your own purpose for attending the meeting. Check in with yourself throughout the discussion – what are you doing to contribute to your purpose? Ask yourself this in relation to each agenda item. So for example, if it's a team meeting and you are new to the team, and your goal is to find out more about the work of others and how it relates to you, then that's the kind of questions you need to be asking. You need to be selective in what actions you take on, but be sure to look for and take opportunities that will allow you to achieve your goals.

7. SAY NO

There will be times when you are tempted to take on an action, or are asked directly if you can do so. It's important to be realistic about what you can take on. It's absolutely OK to say no some of the time. You can do that in different ways, for example by explaining that you don't have the capacity right now, or that you will get back to someone and let them know.

You could also try to negotiate a more realistic deadline, or agree to provide a list of initial thoughts before the next meeting for discussion. By stating clearly what you can and can't do, those at the meeting can decide if that will suffice or if it's better for someone else to take on the task.

8. MAKE SURE ACTIONS ARE CLARIFIED

One of the biggest enemies of productive meetings is vagueness. If things are left undecided, or actions are not crystal clear to everyone around the table, the chances are that things will feel even less clear in a week's time when it comes to the follow-through. One of the best things you can do as a participant in any meeting is bring the specificity: 'You said it would be completed soon – what's the deadline?', 'You've talked about three people working on this together, what's the division of the labour and who is ultimately responsible?', 'What's the most important thing here to get done?', 'How exactly are we expecting to solve this' and so on. Bringing clarity by understanding the specifics of the task is an underrated skill, but in a meeting it's likely to be appreciated.

9. REMEMBER OUR YANG ENERGY – GO DO SOME PRODUCTIVE WORK INSTEAD!

Perhaps the meeting has descended into chaos, everyone is chatting about some very interesting stuff, but it's not interesting to you, or it's not serving the purpose of the meeting. What to do? Our yin instinct is to sit and listen (out of politeness, if nothing else) but our yang

energy is to break out and do something more meaningful and productive with our time.

What you need to weigh up in the moment is a) are you in the wrong meeting – maybe your attendance wasn't the right choice, and b) has the meeting been derailed in some way?

For the first situation, you could say something like: 'Do you still need me for this? I have just remembered that I have to get back to a client/visit the dentist/work on that urgent proposal/other urgent thing that can't wait.'

For the second situation, use phrases along the lines of: 'This is really interesting stuff, but we've moved away from the point here, can we get back to talking about ...' or 'Let's list those things and come back to them later. We were talking about ...'. You don't have to be the chair of the discussion to do this. Many chairs will thank you, and if they disagree they can say so and keep the conversation where it is.

10. QUESTION EVERYTHING

We often fall into auto-pilot mode, so regularly asking ourselves good questions throughout a meeting is important to help us remember our purpose, channel our yang energy and stay on track. Here are a few helpful questions to keep in your mind:

▶ Do I know why I am here? What is my purpose in the meeting?

▶ Do I know everyone – and know the context of what they're bringing to the discussion? Do I need to let the chair know if I need to leave early (or even on time)?

▶ Am I dominating discussion?

▶ Am I listening and taking on board the views of others?

▶ What can I do to support the meeting leaders in their role?

▶ What can I do to make my contribution a useful and positive one?

▶ What can I do to help set or improve the tone of the meeting?

▶ Do I understand all of the jargon being used? If not, how could I best seek clarification?

▶ Have I captured my actions? Am I clear about what needs to be done, when, by who and who needs to know about it?

▶ Is the meeting on track? If not, what can I do to help it get back there?

EXERCISE: STEPPING BACK

What you'll need:
Somewhere to take notes and your meetings calendar

How long it'll take:
20 minutes

Mindset:
Ruthlessness, Preparedness and Zen-Like Calm

Think about the meetings that you have attended, this week, last week, even last year. Which stand out as being good, or not so good? How can you use this knowledge in the future?

Think back to the yin and yang energy of meetings:

▶ Have I got the personal balance right between yin (listening, meeting and connecting) and yang (getting out of meetings to create and get things done).

▶ What about the organisation? Are there too many meetings? Not enough listening and empathy?

▶ How can *my* meetings help restore the balance (we *all* own the culture).

What are some of the techniques in this chapter that I can ...

▶ Try for the first time?

▶ Bring back into my repertoire?

▶ Encourage others to use for particular meetings?

YOU WILL KNOW THAT YOU ARE FIXING MEETINGS WHEN:

▶ You are clear on a meeting's purpose and work to keep this on track, regardless of your role in the meeting.

▶ You are willing to experiment and take unorthodox approaches to achieve the best results and maintain engagement.

▶ You take responsibility for maintaining your energy levels.

5.
AFTER THE MEETING

The goal of every meeting, of course, is to make sure that it runs in a way that encourages productive follow-through. In this chapter we will provide ideas and tips on how to plan and behave during meetings to create change, and encourage this follow-through for all. And if you like what you learn here, then we'd suggest that you head to Graham's book, *How to be a Productivity Ninja*, where you can find loads more ideas and practices to help you get ahead and start feeling great about work again.

IT'S ALL ABOUT SERVICING THE 'AFTER'

Imagine a global summit on an important issue, say climate change. World leaders and experts get together over a period of several days and identify what needs to be done to save our planet. Then they go home and do nothing. What was the point of the summit, the expense, the time that could have been spent doing something else? If nothing changes as a result of your meeting, you made a mistake in having the meeting in the first place. If you have bought into the need for a meeting, you need to be able to prioritise the actions.

REFLECTION ON THE PROCESS OF A MEETING (AS AN ORGANISER)

If the meeting is a regular feature in your diary, spend some time afterwards thinking and reflecting. If it's a weekly meeting, you can perhaps review it monthly – set yourself a reminder. Figure out if the meeting is still needed. If you decide that it is, it's time to consider any ways that it can be improved, for yourself, for your attendees and for achieving your purpose. Matthew Syed in *Black Box Thinking* makes a strong case for why we should look to learn from our experiences and we'd like to encourage you to apply some of that thinking to your meetings. This helps you to make it better for the next time.

DID YOU MEET THE 4 PS?

Remember the 4 Ps from the 'before' chapter? As the meeting organiser you want to see if you got these right. They are:

▶ Purpose

▶ Plan

▶ Protocols

▶ People

PURPOSE
PLAN
PROTOCOL
PEOPLE

DID YOU MEET YOUR PURPOSE?

After your meeting, revisit its purpose. Ask yourself, was it met? If it was, then it sounds like your planning and preparation paid off. If it wasn't, then there is more work to be done. You might want to consider:

▶ Was the purpose the right one for this meeting?

▶ Did the chair keep the discussion on track?

▶ Did the participants contribute to keeping the discussion focused on meeting the purpose?

Once you have started looking at these issues, you can begin to consider what you might do differently next time in order to develop your meeting skills.

YOUR PLAN

Sometimes the best laid plans can go wrong due to unexpected factors. We've all experienced moments like this at work and in life outside of work. Meetings are no exception. Consider:

▶ Did you choose the right format for the meeting?

▶ Did people have the information that they needed in advance so as to best participate in the meeting?

YOUR PROTOCOLS

Consider if your protocols helped people to maximise their energy and attention. If participants spent the session gazing at their mobile phones and found it difficult to focus, then you didn't get that right.

If your meeting was online, did people struggle to engage with the technology? Did people keep dipping in and out? If this was the case, perhaps your protocols need updating or renegotiating.

YOUR PEOPLE

A meeting is made up of people, and it's their contribution that makes it a success or not.

▶ Did you have the right people at your meeting? If not, you might need to engage them now.

▶ Were diverse opinions expressed? A meeting where everyone agrees without discussion, or follows the views of the HiPPO, could be one lacking in diversity of thought (unless perhaps this work has been done outside of the meeting).

▶ Were people fully prepared? If they weren't, perhaps you might need to have some follow-up conversations with them about what you need them to do next time. It's possible that you didn't have the same expectations, so something went wrong in the planning phase. Firing off an email telling someone what you want them to do differently isn't likely to result in changed action, so consider carefully what you know about this person and how they respond to feedback in order to bring about change.

HOW WAS IT FOR YOU?

Having thought about the actions and contributions of others, it's time to consider how you did as the chair or leader. After every delivery of a workshop, Hayley considers how it went from her point of view and identifies something that she will try doing differently next time. This is usually just a small change, such as using a different story or explanation, with the intent to constantly improve her workshops.

Spend a few moments after each meeting thinking about what worked well, and what you might do differently if you were to have the same meeting again. By reflecting, even very briefly, on our own engagement in a meeting, we are striving to improve our involvement, which makes the meeting better for everyone.

EXERCISE: WERE THE 4 PS A SUCCESS?

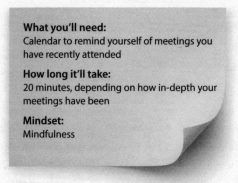

What you'll need:
Calendar to remind yourself of meetings you have recently attended

How long it'll take:
20 minutes, depending on how in-depth your meetings have been

Mindset:
Mindfulness

Cast your mind back to some of the meetings that you have chaired in recent weeks or months. Consider the purpose you set for each meeting and compare that with what was achieved. If the purpose was not met, consider what happened and what you can learn from this.

ASK AROUND

There is nothing wrong with asking your attendees more about how the session was for them, especially if you are new to chairing or you are testing some new approaches in your meetings. If people seemed disengaged, ask them about it. If people didn't contribute, find out why. It could be that people had other things going on, for example if they took part in an online meeting while on the train; if there was a lot of background noise, they may have stayed quieter than usual. As the meeting host or organiser, having a brief chat with some key participants can be really insightful.

As you go down this route, be prepared to hear things you may not like. Listen to that feedback, digest it and use it. Hayley once asked a disengaged member of her team about why she'd not contributed in some team discussions. She told Hayley that this was because she didn't really value what her team members said – she didn't like or respect some of them which meant she couldn't be bothered to interact and debate issues with them. Hayley didn't like what she heard, and needed to think carefully about what to do differently. However, the feedback was very honest – if you can encourage people to speak truthfully, and make it clear that there won't be negative consequences, then you could make your meetings much more successful going forwards.

Following up with participants who seemed disengaged, were involved in moments of tension, or had significant actions, is all part of the role of being the organiser or the chair of the meeting.

WHAT ABOUT AS A PARTICIPANT (NOT A HOST)

Do you ever leave a meeting wondering why on earth you just attended? Do you spend some of the meeting thinking about the work piling up on your desk, wondering why you aren't doing that instead?

It's hard to give your attention to a meeting that isn't meeting your goals. Hopefully by being ruthless about the meetings that you attend, you won't be feeling this way. That's why it's so important to check in with yourself after a meeting, to question if the right choices were made, and to think about how you can improve your energy and input in the future.

Consider these points after every meeting:

▶ Did the meeting achieve its overall purpose? If not, then perhaps there is more you can do to steer from the back seat. Might a guest appearance have been a better way to engage with the bits of the agenda that interested you?

▶ If it's a regular meeting, how will you approach it differently next time?

▶ Think about your contribution. Were you happy that you listened to others? Did you raise the points that you had wanted to? Do you need to do work outside of the meeting to help get others on board with your point of view? How will you go about doing this?

Your goal is to leave each meeting feeling that you have achieved something, that progress was made and that you contributed in a meaningful way. Where this isn't the case, all is not lost. You are in the process of honing your meetings skills, and you will make mistakes in terms of which meetings you attend, how you drive from the back seat and how you contribute. Perfecting meeting skills requires practice and training. Think of your post-meeting reflections as an important element in your training schedule. Be your own coach and decide what you would do differently next time.

> **• REMEMBER •**
>
> If you aren't the meeting chair or organiser, you have decided to attend because you have something to add. By attending, you make it partly your responsibility to make the meeting a success. Reflecting on that is part of your responsibility.

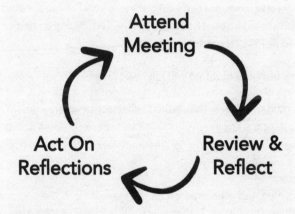

THE POWER OF CLARITY — HOW TO MAKE YOUR MEETINGS ACTION-FOCUSED

One of the things that stands out about good meetings is that they focus on actions. We don't mean running through a list of actions that no one has completed from the last meeting. We mean meetings where the follow-up actions are clear, achievable, and then completed.

PREPARATION, MEETING, ACTION

Remember it's what happens outside of the meeting that makes the difference; the meeting is a vehicle to help you get to where you want to be, rather than the objective itself. If you are running the meeting, you have some level of ownership over the actions. This could mean outlining how you want actions to be recorded and asking people to let you know when their actions have been completed.

A long document of meeting minutes that details verbatim what was said and by whom can be a pretty dull and unproductive read. Minutes should instead be action-orientated, clearly stating what is needed from each participant.

Actions from the meeting will take two forms:

1. A next physical action, which will describe exactly what needs to happen. For example, 'Samir will speak to Gavin about how much budget remains for this year and report back to everyone via email.'

2. A delegated outcome, which will leave it up to the responsible individual to identify their next physical actions themselves. For example, 'Sam will have developed a marketing strategy for the new product.'

You don't need to be the meeting organiser to be able to ask 'Who is going to do that?', 'What's the next physical action' and 'When does that need to be done by?'. The table below shows some examples of how to record next physical actions, and the level of detail required:

Vague action	Next physical action
Jason, budget	Jason to circulate updated budget figures a week before the next meeting, outlining any recommendations based on these numbers
Elaine, induction, marketing	Elaine to include a meeting with Jason within the first two weeks of new marketing manager's induction
Sam, room	Sam to book a bigger meeting room for next meeting
Jack and Jill, launch event	Jack and Jill to agree objectives and budget for launch event for new product and communicate the date to everyone. Jack to then lead on delivering objectives

These next physical actions are clear and specific. Some are more significant pieces of work, but it's easy to see if they have been carried out and there is no room for uncertainty about the person responsible, or those holding them to account. It's also helpful to include when each task should be completed by, and how the individual should report back that it has been done.

For board meetings or more formal meetings, lengthier minutes are often required, but an actions section can still be helpful. This means people can skip to what is most relevant to them without getting lost in the detail.

> **• REMEMBER •**
>
> Use language that outlines each next physical action clearly. Where work is more complex, be sure to outline the expected end result.

THE LAST TEN MINUTES – MAKE SURE YOU GEAR YOUR MEETINGS AROUND THINGS CHANGING

As we talked about earlier in the book, using a bit of stealth and camouflage to put aside ten minutes at the end of the meeting can result in many of the tasks being started straight away. If a task can't be started straight away, there would at least be time for everyone to note their actions and be sure that they know what is needed from them. There might even be time for them to go to the toilet before their next meeting – a luxury for some of the executives that we work with! Could you add ten minutes of 'getting started' time to the end of your meetings?

EXERCISE: MISSION-CRITICAL ACTIONS

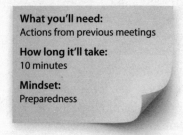

What you'll need:
Actions from previous meetings

How long it'll take:
10 minutes

Mindset:
Preparedness

Take a look at the actions generated from previous meetings. Are there any actions that stand out as being more mission-critical? If so, check in with the person who took that action. You could ask if they have done it yet, and if not, whose help do they need to get it done?

If that person is you, what's stopping you? Think about what you need to do to get this task completed.

TAKE NOTE

Do you ever fail to complete your actions, or complete them at a time that is not right for you, because you are waiting on someone else to send you notes from the meeting? If you don't have your actions in front of you straight away, other deadlines and commitments often get in the way. As an engaged participant, capturing your own actions during a meeting means you are no longer relying on someone else.

But how do you record your actions? We get asked this a lot. Often it's a case of experimenting and trying to find some good habits that work for you. You could use a corner of a notebook, or try Hayley's method of writing a capital A with a circle around it to signify an action. She tries to input these actions into her second brain at the end of the day or straight after the meeting if possible. The backup plan is that these actions get captured in the weekly review (more on this to come later in the chapter).

THE RACE IS ON

Would you appreciate it if every meeting you attended resulted in the actions or minutes being sent to you the same day? How about before you even make it back to your desk? If you are the person taking the notes, you can try a few things to achieve that result. Test them out and see what works for you:

▶ Use a flip chart or a smart board to write every action up as you go along. (You can scan the flip chart using a scanning app or take a picture on your phone. Be aware that an emailed photo can result in the text being difficult for people to see in detail.)

▶ Use OneNote or a shared doc to record the actions. If you are using Microsoft Word, you can email the document as soon as the meeting finishes. As an added bonus, the document could be projected onto the screen in the meeting room or shared online so that everyone can see it as you go along.

If you're the chair, encourage the note-taking to be done in these ways to get the notes to people as quickly as possible, ideally while they are still in the room. Use the last part of the meeting to make sure everyone understands what is expected of them going forwards and how they will report back before the next meeting.

> **• REMEMBER •**
>
> The goal is for everyone's actions to land on their desks before they get back from the meeting.

EVERY ACTION HAS ONE SINGLE OWNER

A shared responsibility often means it's no one's responsibility, or that there will be duplication. Your meeting should allocate actions to individuals. There is no issue with that action then being delegated after the meeting, but the person who takes ownership in the meeting is responsible for making sure that it happens.

DEADLINES AND MILESTONES/EXPECTATIONS

Deadlines help to focus the mind. It is important to seek clarity on them, as they ensure that everyone has the same understanding not just about who will do what, but about when they will do it. Anyone in a meeting can ask about them, not just those with a role in the meeting.

THE POWER OF CLARITY – GOOD PRODUCTIVITY PRINCIPLES TO GET YOUR MEETING ACTIONS DONE

Most of our clients experience having too much work and not enough time, and meetings with many actions simply add to this. Let's look at a few techniques that could help.

SECOND BRAINS

Existing fans of *How to be a Productivity Ninja* will be aware of the importance of capturing and collecting all your next physical actions in your second brain tool – and not only in relation to meetings.

Think Productive's Productivity Ninja Academy contains lots of short videos and resources on how to set up a digital or analog tool in this way. Essentially, a second brain is a resource that is more sophisticated than a to-do list. You create a list of master actions that will allow you to make better decisions throughout the day about what needs to be done next. You will be able to make decisions based on the projects that you are working on, as well as their level of urgency, the level of impact of an action, or your own energy levels throughout the week. Using a second brain tool will give you certainty that you are focusing your attention on the right thing.

PROJECTS VS ACTIONS

Some of the things that need your energy and attention are projects, while others will be next actions. Your projects will be things such as 'Managing the team' or 'Holiday' or 'Develop marketing plan'. As projects, these are not immediate actions for you to cross off your lists. In fact, they will each have a collection of next physical actions that sit underneath them. Getting clear on what is a project and what is a next action will help you move forwards. For each project you will then devise a set of actionable tasks. Some projects will be ongoing, while others will have a specific deadline.

WAITING FOR LIST

As a CEO, Graham used to attend meetings with the whole team, the leadership team and 1-2-1s with staff that he managed. People would agree to do things as a result of these meetings, and Graham would struggle to keep track of who had been tasked with doing what.

Anyone whose role involves working with others will have tasks that they can't move forwards on until others have completed their actions first. Keeping track of these things means that you chase them as needed. You can do this by creating an area in your digital second brain or notebook called 'waiting on others' (see Slice and

Dice below). This is especially important if waiting for someone else's action slows down what you need to do, or if you are the meeting chair and want to follow up on key actions before you meet again.

RENEGOTIATION – CHECKING THAT THE PRIORITIES HAVEN'T CHANGED

Most working environments are fast-paced places, where priorities can change daily. Last week's meeting and the actions that it generated may have to go on a back burner should your organisation be announcing mergers, restructures, client requests and the like. When things change, check out where your actions sit as you get new information about developments happening around you. If your role is more junior, this will involve checking with others that the work still needs to go ahead with the same time scales. If you are in a more senior role, this could be about making conscious decisions about your own priorities and the organisation as a whole, and then communicating this to others.

SLICE AND DICE

Within your second brain, there are different ways that you can organise your actions based on context, such as people, place, your energy levels, or who you have access to. So if you are looking at all of your actions from the past week's meetings, you might notice that six of those involve speaking to other people, and you have decided that this is best done over the phone. You would indicate in your second brain (usually with labels or tags if using an online tool) that these are calls to make.

You can then easily pull up all of the calls that you need to make using your 'calls' label, pick up your phone and get calling people. This allows you to do something that we call batching: grouping together similar tasks, enabling you to move swiftly from one to the next. When this concept was introduced to Hayley, she said that she usually works on a specific project, doing all of the actions that relate to this area of work first. But batching similar tasks together across different projects is in fact an easier way for most people to work. The brain gets into that mode of working, making it faster to complete all of the tasks in that batch.

REVIEW

As Productivity Ninjas we do a weekly review to check in with everyone's actions and ask if we have been spending our attention wisely. It's a chance to ask ourselves if our meetings have been working well for us, and if not, to make some plans about how to change that.

Reviewing the past week's meetings, you could ask yourself some of the following questions:

▶ Have I captured my actions? If not, you could take some time to do so now.

▶ Am I clear on what I need to do to complete those actions?

▶ What help do I need to complete my actions?

▶ What can I delegate?

▶ Can I create some time where I am less likely to be interrupted in order to get this stuff done? Where can I go to do that? (We call this stealth and camouflage.)

▶ Did I participate fully? If not, what happened? How can I do this differently next time?

▶ Are there any discussions I want to follow up on outside of the meeting?

▶ Is there anything I want to raise at the meeting next time, or get on the agenda for the future?

▶ If I was chairing the meeting, how did I do?

▶ Was the meeting useful?

▶ Did it meet my purpose?

If the answer to these last two questions is no, you need to be thinking about your attendance.

The weekly review is also a chance to look ahead to the meetings that you have coming up. It's useful to apply some ruthlessness here, to decide if preparing for them is the best use of your energy and attention this week.

During your review you should be identifying the things that you want to achieve each week, and checking that there is capacity within your schedule to do them. If there isn't, you might need to create some more time, which might mean reducing the time that you spend in meetings.

What you'll need:
Somewhere to take notes, your calendar

How long it'll take:
About 20 minutes

Mindset:
Preparedness

EXERCISE: TIME TO ACT?

Work through the checklist above, thinking about the meetings that you have been to recently. Capture any actions that this generates. If any will take two minutes or less, do them right away.

POWER HOUR

It's likely that your colleagues also have many meetings to go to and actions to complete. How about organising a Power Hour? This could either be with your team, to complete actions from meetings that you attended separately that week, or with people who attended a specific meeting, so you are all working on its actions together.

The idea of a Power Hour is that you all work on something together intensely, bringing a sense of team spirit and possibly some fun. Let's face it, if you have all committed to working on the actions from your meetings at the same time, you are hopefully less likely to be procrastinating on something else.

You start the Power Hour off with either a quick stand-up meeting or online check-in, lasting no more than a few minutes. You agree individually which actions you will work on, then go and do that for one hour. No excuses, no working on something else. You could have a cheer, or something to recognise when one of your actions is complete. Have a definite end to your Power Hour, too. Perhaps making a drink and moving away from the desk, or checking back in online, would be useful.

The purpose is to create a shared experience, to celebrate success and get the work done in short bursts. You could pick an hour each week – at the same time every week, to help gain momentum.

FROGS

Mark Twain talked about eating the frog first thing in the morning. Think of your frog as the task on your to-do list that you least want to do. If you don't do it, you have a bad day because you know you need to do that unpleasant thing later. If you do it first thing, you know that the day is only going to get better. You'll be surprised how the frog is rarely as bad as you think it is going to be. The other thing we like about this approach is that you feel like you have achieved a lot as soon as you have eaten your frog. Identifying which actions are your frogs and doing them first thing will help add momentum to your work.

ACCOUNTABILITY

For some people, having external accountability can be a real motivator. When you agree to own an action, ask who wants to be kept updated on its progress. Or as a chair, it can be helpful to allocate someone to check in with people on their progress.

REALISTIC

In our workshops, we see so many people who have completely unrealistic expectations of what they can get done in a day. If your role is in the driving seat, deciding what's next for your team or organisation, we'd suggest you aim to do no more than five things each day. Write them down at the start of the day, and work on them before you get pulled in different directions. If your role is one that is highly dependent on external factors (which can include your boss piling on the work), don't start the day with an expectation that you will do more than two or perhaps three things. You need to leave yourself some capacity within the day to make sure that you can get any unexpected things done.

If your day is full of meetings (and we hope, by the time you have reached this stage of the book, that it's not), you might need to be kind to yourself and recognise that the meeting itself is work and counts as one of your five things for that day.

YOU WILL KNOW THAT YOU ARE FIXING MEETINGS WHEN:

▶ You reflect on attendance and make changes when needed.

▶ You record next physical actions or desired outcomes for yourself.

▶ As the chair or host, you ensure follow-through by working with others outside of the meeting.

EPILOGUE

As we mentioned at the beginning of this book, in a world of fragmented and often frenetic attention, meetings are unique in their ability to bring people together to share their attention with one another, to listen deeply and to co-operate.

In fact, when you think about it, these are also the things that seem to be lacking from the world: more empathy, collaboration, understanding and respect would be desirable in all kinds of situations. At the highest levels, we need great meetings to push the world forward: climate change conventions, peace treaty negotiations, governmental hearings that decide how to help the poorest and most vulnerable members of society, and pitches to ensure that the brightest new inventors find people willing to take a risk on their world-changing ideas.

It's not far-fetched to say that the future of humanity relies on great meetings.

The world is relying on some of *your* great meetings too. The way you co-operate and collaborate with others will influence people getting jobs, new initiatives being a success, and of course a whole range of seemingly more mundane but no less important things: the happiness and self-esteem of your colleagues, budgets being spent more wisely, creative solutions being found and much more.

We invite you to keep in mind the yin and yang of meetings for yourself and your team, balancing the need for deep listening and deep work: time in meetings listening, learning and contributing, versus time away from meetings, focusing on making things happen.

We hope this book has provided some inspiration, either helping to spark new thinking or perspectives, or to recognise your existing good practices. Over the years, we've seen our share of great meetings and grating meetings. We hope you feel inspired to help us eliminate the unproductive ones – because brilliant meetings are what we need to change the world.

If you'd like to get in touch with us, you can email graham@thinkproductive.co.uk or hayley@thinkproductive.co.uk – we'd be delighted to hear your stories.

Graham Allcott
Hayley Watts
2020

When all else fails, keep yourself entertained with our meetings bullsh*t bingo.

WIN WIN	YOUR CONNECTION IS UNSTABLE	MOVING THE GOAL POSTS	TOUCH BASE
MOBILE PHONE INTERRUPTION	ASAP	SCALEABLE	FILL ME/THEM IN
GET THE BALL ROLLING	LET'S SET UP ANOTHER MEETING	NO BRAINER	WE CAN'T HEAR YOU, YOU'RE ON MUTE
AGILE	FUTURE PROOF	HIT THE GROUND RUNNING	AT THE END OF THE DAY

Add in your own commonly used TLAs (Three Letter Acronyms) and jargon.

WIN WIN	BENCH MARK	MOVING THE GOAL POSTS	
	ASAP		FILL ME/THEM IN
GET THE BALL ROLLING		NO BRAINER	BACK TO THE DRAWING BOARD
		HIT THE GROUND RUNNING	

There are even tools online to generate your own bingo games for meetings!

NOTES

Chapter 1

1. 'Stop the Meeting Madness' by Leslie A. Perlow, Constance Noonan Hadley and Eunice Eun, *Harvard Business Review*, July–August 2017: https://hbr.org/2017/07/stop-the-meeting-madness

2. The *Wall Street Journal* quoted in Hubspot, 'You're Going to Waste 31 Hours in Meetings This Month', Corey Wainwright, 12th June 2014: https://www.wsj.com/articles/the-science-of-better-meetings-11550246239

3. 'The Mere Presence of Your Smartphone Reduces Brain Power, Study Shows', UT News, 26th June 2017: https://news.utexas.edu/2017/06/26/the-mere-presence-of-your-smartphone-reduces-brain-power/

4. 'Cell Phone Alerts May Be Driving you to Distraction', Florida State University, 9th July 2015: https://www.fsu.edu/indexTOFStory.html?lead.distraction

5. 'Stress of Modern Life Cuts Attention Span to Five Minutes', *The Telegraph*: https://www.telegraph.co.uk/news/health/news/3522781/Stress-of-modern-life-cuts-attention-spans-to-five-minutes.html

6. 'Why is Being Alone with our Thoughts so Hard?', David DiSalvo, *Psychology Today*, 9th August 2014: https://www.psychologytoday.com/us/blog/neuronarrative/201408/why-is-being-alone-our-thoughts-so-hard

Chapter 2

1. Chairs and facilitators are also participants!

2. 'The Power of the Word "Because" to Get People to Do Stuff', Susan Weinschenk Ph.D., *Psychology Today*, 15th October 2013: https://www.psychologytoday.com/us/blog/brain-wise/201310/the-power-the-word-because-get-people-do-stuff

Chapter 3

1. https://en.wikipedia.org/wiki/User_experience_design

2. 'What is UX Design? 15 User Experience Design Experts Weigh In': https://www.usertesting.com/blog/what-is-ux-design-15-user-experience-experts-weigh-in/

3. 'What is the UX Design Process? (2019)' https://www.youtube.com/watch?v=Um3BhY0oS2c

4. 'A Profile of Meetings In Corporate America: Results of the 3M Meeting Effectiveness Study', Monge, P.R., McSween, C., & Wyer, J., Annenberg School of Communications, University of Southern California, Los Angeles: https://ceo.usc.edu/1989/11/22/a-profile-of-meetings-in-corporate-america-results-of-the-3m-meeting-effectiveness-study/

5. 'Why Jeff Bezos Makes Amazon Execs Read 6-page Memos at the Start of Each Meeting', cnbc.com: https://www.cnbc.com/2018/04/23/what-jeff-bezos-learned-from-requiring-6-page-memos-at-amazon.html

6. 'The Power of Introverts', Susan Cain, TED2019: https://www.ted.com/talks/susan_cain_the_power_of_introverts?language=en

7. 'Surprise! We're Multitasking Too Much During Meetings', tech.co: https://tech.co/news/surprise-multitasking-much-meetings-infographic-2014-11

8. 'This is Your Brain on Multitasking', Garth Sundem, *Psychology Today*, 24th February 2012: https://www.psychologytoday.com/us/blog/brain-trust/201202/is-your-brain-multitasking

NOTES

9. 'Doodle Presents: The State of Meetings Report 2019': https://en.blog.doodle.com/2019/01/10/pointless-meetings-will-cost-companies-530bn-in-2019/
10. 'The Importance of Small Team Size': http://flow-state.blogspot.com/2012/01/importance-of-small-team-size.html
11. 'A Silent Meeting is Worth a Thousand Words': https://medium.com/square-corner-blog/a-silent-meeting-is-worth-a-thousand-words-2c7213b12fb6

Chapter 4

1. https://www.virgin.com/entrepreneur/infographic-the-importance-of-face-to-face-networking
2. Danziger, S., Levav, J., & Avnaim-Pesso, L., 'Extraneous factors in judicial decisions', *PNAS*, 2011: https://doi.org/10.1073/pnas.1018033108
3. Bluedorn, A. C., Turban, D. B., & Love, M. S. (1999), The effects of stand-up and sit-down meeting formats on meeting outcomes', *Journal of Applied Psychology*, *84*(2), 277–285, https://doi.org/10.1037/0021-9010.84.2.277
4. 'Spanx on Steroids: How Speedo Created the New Record-Breaking Swimsuit': https://www.smithsonianmag.com/science-nature/spanx-on-steroids-how-speedo-created-the-new-record-breaking-swimsuit-9662/?c=y&story=fullsto
5. 'Doodlers, Unite!', Sunni Brown, TED2011: https://www.ted.com/talks/sunni_brown_doodlers_unite?language=en
6. 'What does Doodling do?', Jackie Andrade, *Applied Cognitive Psychology*: http://pignottia.faculty.mjc.edu/math134/homework/doodlingCaseStudy.pdf

ACKNOWLEDGEMENTS

GRAHAM AND HAYLEY WOULD LIKE TO THANK ...

We'd both like to say a huge thanks to our editor Ellen for her patience, constructive ideas and for helping us to make this a better book. We'd like to thank our fellow meetings travellers in the global community at Think Productive.

Thank you to our focus group participants, many of whom are friends from across the years, and as far afield as New Zealand, California, Oxfordshire and Surrey. Your time and constructive feedback was appreciated and reminded us how many wonderful people we have in our lives: Cara Delaney, Sophie Devonshire, Laila Motty, Suzanne Pullman, Grace Marshall, Joanne Hulbert, Jane Newman, Glenda Sinclair, Dan Bromley, Lucy Barber, Nicola Manuel, Mark Ibison, Russell Brooks, Ed Montgomery and Lloyd Clark.

HAYLEY WOULD LIKE TO THANK ...

Tim Robins and Emma Howes for encouraging me to do this project. I have cursed you many times, and appreciate your confidence in me and encouraging me to have a go. Tim, I appreciate your reading and correcting my spelling and grammar in my writing over the years. I'm sure it's been painful, but I appreciate your help.

Claire Farr for encouraging me and reminding me that we will celebrate with Prosecco when this work is done. This has kept me going on so many different occasions. Your tireless support of my latest endeavours is helped by knowing you will always cheer me up and make me laugh.

Russell Brooks and Nigel Robinson for showing me that meetings can be well run, and that the chairperson can make a difference to the meetings and actions taken as a result. I learned a lot from you both. To Matthew Brown and Martin Farrell whose work encouraged me to challenge meetings and showed me there was a better way.

To Graham for having the patience to help me, explain endlessly how it's done and for keeping an eye on the detail. To Cara for her unwavering support in updating our meetings workshops and getting excited about this with me, I'm sure it will spread further afield soon.

GRAHAM WOULD LIKE TO THANK ...

Hayley, thanks for bringing such energy to this topic – both in the collaboration for this book and more widely for Think Productive's meetings offering. Thanks also for putting up with me being slack with some of our internal deadlines when I was brain-dead and numb to the words on the screen.

Thanks to Martin Farrell, Christopher Spence, Fiona Dawe, Max McLoughlin, Julia Poole, Penny Francis, Sir Stuart Etherington, Elena Kerrigan and many others for helping me to get my own meetings right.

And to Cara, Jess, Caitlin, Lee, Grace, Matthew and the rest of the Think Productive family – thanks for helping bring all this to life for our clients as we change the world one humble meeting at a time.

Finally, thank you to Elise for looking after Roscoe a few times in the middle of the Covid crisis, freeing up my time to get the edits done.

APPENDIX

THINK PRODUCTIVE

Think Productive runs a range of practical productivity workshops including:

▶ How to be a Productivity Ninja (full day implementation)

▶ The Way of the Productivity Ninja (short keynote session)

▶ Getting Your Inbox to Zero

▶ Fixing Meetings

▶ Supercharge Your Virtual Meetings

▶ Chair Meetings Like a Productivity Ninja

Graham and Hayley are available for keynote talks.

Go to **www.thinkproductive.com**
for more details
or email **hello@thinkproductive.com**
to find out more.

FIXING MEETINGS WORKSHOPS

So you've fixed all your own meetings, but what about Dave from accounts?! Perhaps we can help.

If you want to change meeting culture in your organization, Think Productive runs a range of in-house workshops to do exactly that. We started in the UK and are now making our way around the world too:

FIXING MEETINGS

Helping you to reduce how much time you spend in meetings, and making the meetings that you do attend ridiculously productive. Participants leave with a set of practical tools to help them have better meetings and to positively challenge the culture of their organization's meeting addictions.

Part of the session involves making practical changes to real meetings (not just working on case study examples) so that changes are made on the day.

CHAIR MEETINGS LIKE A PRODUCTIVITY NINJA

Making meetings more productive and effective, and a pleasure to take part in. Learn how to overcome human, organizational and practical barriers to delivering effective meetings.

SUPERCHARGE YOUR VIRTUAL MEETINGS

Helping you to reduce the amount of time you spend in meetings, and making the online meetings that you do attend engaging and productive. Participants leave with a set of practical tools to help them have better meetings, and to positively challenge the culture of their organization's meeting addictions.

For more info on our workshops, head to:

www.thinkproductive.com

To find out about bringing our workshops to your company,

email us: hello@thinkproductive.com

Join us on LinkedIn

Follow us on Twitter

Think Productive –
Proc  njas

@grahamallcott
@thin ctive

BEYOND BUSY
WITH GRAHAM ALLCOTT

Graham Allcott is your host for the **business podcast** that asks the big questions. He explores the relationships and tensions between productivity, work/life balance and how humans define happiness and success. Through in-depth interviews with founders, CEOs, sports-people and professional clowns, you'll pick up tips and tricks, inspiration and reading-list suggestions, as well as spending time with interesting people in your ears.

Search 'Beyond Busy' in your podcast app or go to **www.getbeyondbusy.com** to get the latest episodes.

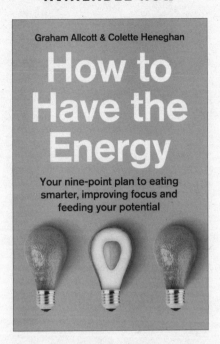